"HOW TO BE CHRISTLIKE"

A JOURNEY OF FAITH, TRANSFORMATION, AND LEGACY

MICHAEL STEVENS

Chapter One Publishing
Company L.L.C.

CONTENTS

PREFACE

~

As I write this preface, I am filled with a profound sense of gratitude and humility. "How to Be Christlike" is more than a book; it is a journey I have been privileged to embark upon alongside many incredible individuals. This book is the culmination of years of personal reflection, study, and, most importantly, living out the principles of Christlikeness in daily life.

In a world that often feels fragmented and chaotic, Jesus Christ's timeless teachings are a beacon of hope and a call to a higher way of living. The path to Christlikeness is not easy, but it promises deep fulfillment, profound peace, and transformative power. It calls us to look beyond ourselves, serve others with humility and love, and live with integrity and grace.

Throughout this book, you will find insights and practical steps that I have gathered from Scripture, personal experiences, and the wisdom of fellow believers. Each chapter is designed to equip you with practical tools to guide you deeper into the heart of what it means to be Christlike, offering both theological reflections and actionable practices.

I owe a particular debt of gratitude to my brothers of Walk 125. Your unwavering support, encouragement, and fellowship have been instrumental in my faith journey. Together, we have faced challenges, celebrated victories, and grown in understanding what it means to follow Christ. This book is dedicated to you with deep appreciation and love.

To the readers of this book, whether you are new to the Christian faith or have been walking with Christ for many years, I hope that you will find this book to be a valuable companion on your journey. May it inspire you to pursue a deeper relationship with Jesus, embody His virtues daily, and impact the world with His love and grace.

The journey toward Christlikeness is a lifelong pursuit, a commitment to continuous growth, perseverance through trials, and an ever-deepening relationship with God. As you read these pages, may you be encouraged to commit to this journey with all your heart, knowing that you are not alone? The Holy Spirit empowers you, the Scriptures guide you, and the community of believers supports you.

May this book inspire and transform you. May it challenge you to reflect Christ in all you do and leave a legacy of faith that impacts future generations. Thank you for allowing me to be a part of your journey.

With heartfelt gratitude,

Michael Stevens

REVIEWS OF PRAISE FOR MICHAEL STEVENS AND "HOW TO BE CHRISTLIKE"

Reviews of Praise

"Michael Stevens is an author on fire for God, and it shows in every page of 'How to Be Christlike.' His passionate and insightful writing offers readers a powerful guide to living a life that mirrors Jesus.

This book is a testament to Stevens' deep faith and dedication to helping others grow spiritually."

— **Samuel Harris, Bestselling Author of 'Ignite Your Faith'**

"Michael Stevens has created a masterful guide to living a Christ-centered life. 'How to Be Christlike' offers profound insights and practical wisdom, making it an essential read for anyone seeking to deepen their faith."

— **Dr. Elizabeth Harper, Theologian and Author**

"This book is a true treasure. Stevens' ability to blend theological depth with practical application is remarkable. 'How to Be Christlike' is both inspiring and transformative."

— **Pastor David Thompson, Senior Pastor, Grace Community Church**

"A must-read for every Christian. Michael Stevens provides a clear and compelling roadmap for living a life that reflects the teachings of Jesus. Highly recommended!"

— **Rebecca Moore, Christian Blogger and Influencer**

"Stevens' writing is both engaging and enlightening. 'How to Be Christlike' is filled with valuable insights that will impact readers' lives profoundly. An excellent resource for personal and spiritual growth."

— **John Carter, Author of 'Faith in Action'**

"This book deeply moved me. Michael Stevens has a unique gift for making complex theological concepts accessible and relatable. 'How to Be Christlike' is an invaluable guide for anyone on a spiritual journey."

— **Emily Davis, Christian Educator**

"A beautifully written and deeply insightful book. Stevens' passion for Christlikeness shines through every page. This guide will benefit believers at any stage of their faith journey."
— **Mark Johnson, Speaker and Podcaster**

"In 'How to Be Christlike,' Michael Stevens provides readers with a comprehensive and practical guide to living out their faith. This book is a testament to the transformative power of Christ's teachings."
— **Sarah Williams, Professor of Theology**

"Stevens has written a masterpiece that combines scholarly research with heartfelt devotion. 'How to Be Christlike' is an inspiring read that challenges and encourages readers to grow in their faith."
— **James Miller, Author, and Spiritual Mentor**

"An essential addition to any Christian's library. Michael Stevens offers profound wisdom and practical steps for living a life that truly reflects the love and teachings of Jesus."
— **Laura Bennett, Christian Life Coach**

"I highly recommend 'How to Be Christlike' to anyone seeking to deepen their relationship with God. Stevens' profound and practical insights make this book a valuable resource for spiritual growth."
— **Daniel Roberts, Pastor, and Author**

"Michael Stevens' book is a beacon of light for those looking to live Christlike lives. His blend of theological depth and practical advice makes 'How to Be Christlike' an indispensable guide for believers."
— **Rachel Adams, Christian Writer and Speaker**

"A truly transformative read. Stevens' thoughtful and engaging approach to Christlikeness gives readers the tools to grow in their faith and impact the world around them."

— **Timothy Anderson, Church Leader**

"Stevens has crafted a book that is both theologically rich and practically useful. 'How to Be Christlike' is an inspiring guide to help readers navigate their spiritual journeys confidently and gracefully."

— **Victoria Hill, Christian Counselor**

"An enlightening and empowering book. Michael Stevens' 'How to Be Christlike' is a valuable resource for anyone looking to live out their faith in a meaningful and impactful way."

— **Brian Matthews, Pastor and Educator**

INTRODUCTION - THE CALL TO CHRISTLIKENESS

~

Embracing Christlike Living

I n a world often besieged by discord, disillusionment, and division, the timeless figure of Jesus Christ emerges as a beacon of hope and an exemplar of love. His life, teachings, and profound impact transcend the boundaries of time and culture, resonating with seekers of truth and righteousness across generations. As we embark on the journey of exploring what it truly means to be Christlike, we are not merely delving into the pages of history but engaging with a living legacy that continues to shape the hearts and minds of millions around the globe.

THE ENDURING relevance of Jesus Christ amidst the complexities of modernity is a testament to the universality and timelessness of his message. In an age characterized by rapid technological advancement, shifting social norms, and geopolitical upheaval, the quest for meaning and purpose remains a fundamental aspect of the human experience. In this quest, the figure of Jesus Christ emerges as a guiding light—a symbol of unwavering faith, boundless compassion, and transformative love.

THE LIFE OF JESUS CHRIST, as chronicled in the Gospels, is a testament to the power of humility, service, and self-sacrifice. Born into humble circumstances in the backwaters of ancient Palestine, Jesus defied the expectations of his time, challenging the religious and political authorities of his day with his radical teachings of love and forgiveness. His ministry, marked by healing, compassion, and inclusion, drew multitudes from all walks of life, transcending the barriers of ethnicity, social status, and religious affiliation.

CENTRAL to the teachings of Jesus Christ is the concept of agape love —a selfless, unconditional love that seeks the well-being and flourishing of others. In a world often characterized by selfishness, greed, and tribalism, the message of love espoused by Jesus stands in stark contrast, offering a vision of human solidarity and kinship that transcends the narrow confines of self-interest. This radical vision of love calls us to embrace the other, to extend compassion to the marginalized and disenfranchised, and to work tirelessly for justice and reconciliation in a world torn asunder by strife and conflict.

THE TRANSFORMATIVE POWER OF JESUS' message is evidenced by the countless lives touched and transformed throughout history. From the early followers who spread the gospel throughout the Roman Empire to the modern-day missionaries who continue to carry the message of hope to the farthest corners of the earth, the influence of Jesus Christ knows no bounds. His teachings have inspired movements for social justice, efforts to alleviate suffering, and initiatives to promote peace and reconciliation in societies torn apart by violence and oppression.

As WE GRAPPLE with the complexities of the modern world, the figure of Jesus Christ offers a timeless example of moral clarity and spiritual resilience. His life reminds us that true greatness is not measured by wealth, power, or status but by the depth of one's character and the extent of one's compassion. In a society often obsessed with material success and superficial accolades, Jesus's teachings challenge us to reevaluate our priorities and strive for a more meaningful and fulfilling existence.

THE ENDURING legacy of Jesus Christ as a beacon of hope and exemplar of love continues to resonate with seekers of truth and righteousness across the globe. As we explore what it truly means to be Christlike, we are invited to delve deeper into his character's essence and emulate his daily virtues. In doing so, we become partakers in a legacy that transcends time and culture, shaping the hearts and minds of future generations.

THE IMPACT OF JESUS' teachings is not confined to any particular era or geographical location; it reverberates through the corridors of history, inspiring individuals to strive for a higher ideal and to live lives of purpose and meaning. From the humblest peasant to the most exalted monarch, from the bustling streets of ancient Jerusalem to the remote villages of Africa and Asia, the message of Jesus Christ has touched hearts and transformed lives in ways that defy human comprehension.

ONE OF THE most remarkable aspects of Jesus' legacy is its capacity to adapt and evolve with the changing tides of history. Despite the passage of millennia, his teachings continue to speak to the deepest longings of the human soul, offering solace to the weary, hope to the oppressed, and a vision of a better world to come. Whether in times of peace or times of turmoil, the message of Jesus Christ remains a steadfast anchor in a sea of uncertainty, guiding humanity toward a brighter future.

THE ENDURING relevance of Jesus Christ in the modern world is best exemplified by the countless individuals and communities who continue to draw inspiration from his life and teachings. From charitable organizations that provide aid to the needy to grassroots movements that advocate for social justice and equality, the influence of Jesus Christ is palpable in every corner of the globe. His love, compassion, and forgiveness message catalyzes positive change, motivating people to reach across race, religion, and nationality boundaries to build a more just and compassionate society.

As WE REFLECT on Jesus Christ's enduring legacy, let us be inspired by his example and strive to emulate his virtues in our own lives. Let us seek to embody the spirit of love, compassion, and humility that characterized his earthly ministry, and let us work together to create a world where justice and peace reign supreme. In doing so, we honor Jesus Christ's legacy and fulfill the timeless mandate to love one another as he loved us.

∾

The Call to Christlikeness

THE CALL to Christlikeness invites us to align our lives with Jesus Christ's teachings and example. It is a call to transcend the world's superficial pursuits and embrace a higher standard of morality and character. Christlikeness encompasses virtues such as love, compassion, humility, and integrity—qualities that reflect the essence of Jesus' character. While the journey toward Christlikeness may be challenging, it is ultimately rewarding, leading to a more profound sense of purpose and fulfillment.

TO FULLY APPRECIATE the significance of this call, we must first understand the profound nature of Jesus' teachings and the life he led. Jesus' message was radical in its simplicity and depth, challenging the prevailing norms of his time and inviting his followers to adopt a new way of living. For instance, his Sermon on the Mount encapsulates the essence of Christlike living, offering timeless principles that continue to guide and inspire believers. Jesus' teachings on love, forgiveness, and service are not mere ideals but practical imperatives that demand a fundamental transformation of our hearts and minds.

LOVE, as Jesus taught, is the cornerstone of Christlikeness. It is a love that goes beyond mere affection or sentimentality; it is a self-less, sacrificial love that seeks the well-being of others above our own. This agape love is exemplified in Jesus' willingness to lay down his life for humanity, offering the ultimate act of love and redemption. To emulate this love is to open our hearts to others, to practice empathy and kindness, and to extend grace even to those who may not deserve it. In a world often driven by self-interest and division, the call to love as Jesus loved is a challenge and a beacon of hope.

COMPASSION, another central virtue of Christlikeness, involves a deep awareness of and responsiveness to the suffering of others. Jesus' ministry was marked by acts of kindness—healing the sick, feeding the hungry, and comforting the brokenhearted. To be Christlike is to cultivate a heart that is moved by the pain and needs of others, prompting us to take tangible steps to alleviate suffering. This requires us to look beyond our circumstances and to recognize the humanity in everyone we encounter, fostering a spirit of generosity and service.

HUMILITY, as demonstrated by Jesus, is the foundation of true greatness. Despite his divine nature, Jesus chose to live a life of humility, associating with the lowly and serving others without seeking recognition or praise. He washed his disciples' feet, a profound act of humility and service that underscores the importance of placing others before ourselves. Embracing humility means acknowledging our limitations, valuing the contributions of others, and rejecting the pursuit of power and status. It calls us to lead with gentleness and serve with a heart free from pride and arrogance.

INTEGRITY, A HALLMARK OF JESUS' character, is about living a life of authenticity and moral uprightness. Jesus embodied integrity in every aspect of his life, remaining steadfast in his commitment to truth and righteousness, even in the face of persecution. To be Christlike, we must uphold these same standards of integrity, ensuring that our actions align with our beliefs and that we live transparently and honestly. Integrity demands consistency in our ethical conduct, fostering trust and respect in our relationships and communities.

THE JOURNEY toward Christlikeness is not without its challenges. It requires a continual process of self-examination, repentance, and growth. We must be willing to confront our flaws and weaknesses, seek forgiveness when we fall short and strive earnestly to embody the virtues of Christ. This journey is not a solitary endeavor; it is nurtured within the community of believers, where we can support, encourage, and hold one another accountable.

MOREOVER, the path to Christlikeness is profoundly personal and transformative. As we align our lives with Jesus's teachings, we experience a profound shift in our perspective and priorities. We begin to see the world through Christ's love and compassion, which influences our decisions and interactions. This transformation brings a more profound sense of purpose as we realize that our lives are part of a larger divine narrative. We find fulfillment not in accumulating wealth or accolades but in the joy of serving others and living out our faith authentically.

ULTIMATELY, the rewards of striving for Christlikeness extend beyond personal fulfillment. We become agents of change as we grow in love, compassion, humility, and integrity. Our lives are a testament to the transformative power of Jesus' teachings, inspiring others to seek the same path. In a world desperately needing hope and healing, the call to Christlikeness is a powerful reminder of the potential for goodness and grace within each of us.

THE CALL to Christlikeness is an invitation to embark on a transformative journey that aligns our lives with the teachings and example of Jesus Christ. It challenges us to rise above superficial pursuits and embrace a higher standard of morality and character, encompassing love, compassion, humility, and integrity. While the journey may be challenging, it is ultimately rewarding, leading to a more profound sense of purpose and fulfillment and enabling us to make a meaningful impact. As we strive to be Christlike, we honor the legacy of Jesus and contribute to the healing and renewal of our communities and the world at large.

Understanding the Importance of Emulating Christ

THE IMPORTANCE of emulating Christ cannot be overstated in a world marked by moral ambiguity and ethical relativism. As followers of Christ, we are called to be ambassadors of his love and grace, demonstrating his teachings through our words and actions. By embodying Christ's virtues, we witness his transformative power and contribute to restoring brokenness and reconciling humanity. Through our emulation of Christ, we become vessels of hope and agents of change in a world needing healing.

IN TODAY'S SOCIETY, the lines between right and wrong are often blurred, and the absolutes of moral truth are frequently questioned or dismissed. This environment of moral ambiguity can lead to confusion, despair, and a sense of purposelessness. In such a context, the clear and unwavering moral teachings of Jesus Christ offer a beacon of light and a source of clarity. Christ's teachings provide a definitive guide for living a life of integrity, compassion, and justice. By adhering to these principles, we can navigate the complexities of modern life with confidence and conviction.

THE ROLE of a Christ follower is to be a living testament to the principles and values that Jesus exemplified. This role transcends mere verbal proclamation of faith; it requires active, tangible demonstration of Christ's love and grace in our daily interactions. Whether in our personal relationships, professional environments, or public engagements, our actions should consistently reflect the teachings of Jesus. This means showing kindness to marginalized people, practicing forgiveness towards those who have wronged us, and advocating for justice in the face of oppression.

EMULATING Christ involves a deep and ongoing commitment to personal and spiritual growth. It requires us to constantly examine our motives, attitudes, and behaviors in light of Christ's example. This process of self-reflection and transformation is not easy, but it is essential for genuine discipleship. By continually striving to align our lives with Christ's teachings, we become more effective witnesses to his love and power. Our lives, then, become a testament to the transformative impact of the Gospel, inspiring others to seek the same path of righteousness and grace.

THE IMPACT of embodying Christ's virtues extends beyond our personal lives; it can potentially effect significant positive change in the broader community and society. When we act with Christlike love and compassion, we contribute to the healing and restoration of broken relationships and fractured communities. Our commitment to justice and mercy can challenge and change unjust systems and structures, bringing more significant equity and harmony. In a world rife with division and conflict, our actions as Christ's ambassadors can promote peace and reconciliation, bridging gaps and building bridges of understanding and cooperation.

MOREOVER, the virtues of Christ that we strive to emulate—love, compassion, humility, and integrity—are universal in their appeal and relevance. They resonate with people of all backgrounds and beliefs, offering a common ground upon which we can build relationships and foster mutual respect. By embodying these virtues, we can transcend the barriers that divide us, such as race, religion, and nationality, and work towards a more inclusive and compassionate world.

THE RESTORATION of brokenness and the reconciliation of humanity are central to the mission of Christ and, by extension, to the mission of his followers. Jesus' ministry was characterized by acts of healing and reconciliation—healing the sick, restoring sight to the blind, and reconciling sinners to God. As his followers, we are called to continue this work of healing and reconciliation in our contexts. This means addressing the physical, emotional, and spiritual needs of those around us and working toward restoring justice and peace in our communities and beyond.

IN PRACTICAL TERMS, this could involve volunteering our time and resources to help those in need, advocating for policies that promote social justice and equity, and fostering environments of inclusivity and respect in our workplaces and social circles. It means being present, offering support to hurting people, and actively seeking ways to promote reconciliation and understanding in conflict situations. Through these actions, we can help heal our world's wounds and contribute to building God's kingdom on earth.

THE IMPORTANCE of emulating Christ in a world marked by moral ambiguity and ethical relativism cannot be overstated. As followers of Christ, we are called to be ambassadors of his love and grace, demonstrating his teachings through our words and actions. By embodying Christ's virtues, we witness his transformative power and contribute to restoring brokenness and reconciling humanity. Through our emulation of Christ, we become vessels of hope and agents of change, offering a much-needed source of healing and renewal in our world. The journey toward Christlikeness is challenging but profoundly rewarding, leading to a more profound sense of purpose and fulfillment as we align our lives with the ultimate example of love, compassion, and integrity.

∼

The Purpose of This Book

"How to Be Christlike" provides a roadmap for individuals seeking to deepen their understanding of Christ's character and emulate his virtues in their daily lives. This book offers guidance on cultivating Christlike qualities such as love, compassion, humility, and integrity through biblical wisdom, theological reflection, and practical insights. Whether you are a seasoned believer seeking spiritual growth or someone exploring the Christian faith for the first time, this book serves as a resource for personal transformation and spiritual enrichment.

At the heart of this journey is a commitment to understanding who Jesus was and how his teachings can be integrated into our modern lives. Christ's character is multifaceted, encompassing a range of virtues that together create a model of perfect humanity. Jesus' life provides a blueprint for living with purpose and grace, regardless of our challenges. This book aims to break down these aspects of Jesus' character into practical steps that can be applied to everyday situations.

One of the foundational elements of Christ's character is love. Jesus taught that love is the greatest commandment, urging us to love God with all our heart, soul, mind, and strength and to love our neighbors as ourselves. This book delves into what it means to truly love in the way Jesus loved—unconditionally and sacrificially. It explores how we can practice this kind of love in our interactions with family, friends, and strangers, creating a ripple effect of kindness and compassion in our communities.

Compassion, closely related to love, is another critical quality that Jesus embodied. His ministry was marked by numerous acts of compassion, from healing the sick to comforting the bereaved. This book provides practical advice on how we can develop a compassionate heart that is attuned to the needs and suffering of others. It encourages readers to take action, whether through small acts of kindness or more significant commitments to social justice, to make a tangible difference in those around us.

HUMILITY IS YET another cornerstone of Christ's character. Despite his divine nature, Jesus lived a life of service and humility, washing his disciples' feet and associating with the marginalized. This book explores the transformative power of humility, offering insights into how we can cultivate this virtue in our own lives. It challenges us to put aside pride and selfishness, serve others selflessly, and find true greatness in lifting others.

INTEGRITY, defined by consistency in moral and ethical principles, is also an essential attribute of Christlikeness. Jesus' unwavering commitment to truth and righteousness set a powerful example for his followers. In this book, readers will find strategies for living with integrity, ensuring that their actions align with their beliefs and that they remain steadfast in their commitment to doing what is right, even when it is difficult.

BEYOND THESE CORE VIRTUES, "How to Be Christlike" also addresses other important aspects of Jesus' character, such as forgiveness, patience, and faith. Each chapter is designed to provide a comprehensive understanding of these qualities, supported by scriptural references and real-life examples. The book emphasizes that emulating Christ is not about perfection but striving to reflect his love and grace in our imperfect lives.

. . .

THIS BOOK's structure is intended to facilitate both individual and group study. Each chapter includes reflection questions and practical exercises to help readers apply their knowledge. Whether used in personal devotions, small group discussions, or church study programs, this book aims to foster meaningful engagement with Jesus's teachings and inspire lasting change.

FOR SEASONED BELIEVERS, "How to Be Christlike" offers a fresh perspective on familiar teachings, encouraging deeper reflection and a renewed commitment to living out one's faith. It reminds readers that the journey of faith is continuous and that there is always room for growth and improvement. For those new to the Christian faith, this book provides an accessible introduction to the core principles of Christlikeness, helping to lay a strong foundation for their spiritual journey.

ULTIMATELY, "HOW TO BE CHRISTLIKE" aims to equip readers with the tools and insights needed to transform their lives and the lives of those around them. By embracing Christ's virtues, we can become agents of positive change, bringing hope, healing, and reconciliation to a needy world. This book invites readers to embark on a transformative journey that leads to a deeper relationship with God and a more profound impact on the world.

"HOW TO BE CHRISTLIKE" serves as a comprehensive guide for anyone seeking to emulate the character of Jesus in their daily lives. This book offers valuable guidance on cultivating love, compassion, humility, integrity, and other Christlike qualities through biblical wisdom, theological reflection, and practical insights. It is a resource designed to inspire personal transformation and spiritual enrichment, helping readers to live out their faith with purpose and grace.

~

How to Use This Book

THIS BOOK IS DESIGNED to be a companion on your journey toward Christlikeness, offering inspiration and practical guidance for your spiritual growth. Each chapter explores a specific aspect of Christ's character, providing insights, reflections, and practical exercises to help you integrate these virtues into your life. Whether you read this book individually or as part of a group study, I encourage you to approach it with an open heart and a willingness to engage deeply with the material. Take time to reflect on the questions, journal your thoughts and experiences, and seek opportunities to put the principles into practice in your daily interactions.

As WE DELVE into the various aspects of Christ's character, you will find that each chapter is meticulously crafted to help you under-stand and embody these virtues meaningfully. For example, when exploring the virtue of love, the chapter will guide you through the profound and selfless love that Jesus exemplified. You will be encouraged to examine your capacity for love, identify areas where you can grow, and actively practice acts of love in your daily life. Reflection questions will prompt you to consider how love mani-fests in your relationships and how you can more fully embody Christ's love in your interactions with others.

. . .

Similarly, when focusing on compassion, the book will provide biblical examples of Jesus' compassionate actions and offer practical advice on cultivating a heart of compassion. Exercises include volunteering at a local charity, reaching out to someone in need, or practicing active listening with those around you. The goal is to move beyond theoretical understanding to real-world application, allowing the teachings of Jesus to transform your life from the inside out.

The chapter on humility will challenge you to reframe your understanding of greatness and service. Drawing on Jesus' example of washing his disciples' feet, you will be invited to consider ways to serve others selflessly without seeking recognition or reward. Practical exercises will encourage you to practice humility in everyday situations, such as giving others credit for their contributions, admitting mistakes, and putting others' needs before your own.

Integrity, another cornerstone of Christlikeness, will be explored by examining Jesus' unwavering commitment to truth and righteousness. You will be prompted to reflect on your values and to assess whether your actions align with your beliefs. Exercises in this chapter include setting personal boundaries, being honest in your communications, and standing up for what is right, even when it is difficult.

Throughout the book, the emphasis will be on practical application and personal reflection. Each chapter will conclude with action steps designed to help you live out the virtues of Christ in tangible ways. Journaling prompts and reflection questions will accompany these steps to encourage deeper introspection and ongoing growth.

Whether engaging with the material individually or as part of a group, these tools will help you internalize the teachings and make meaningful changes in your life.

GROUP STUDY SETTINGS offer additional benefits, as they provide a supportive community where you can share your experiences, learn from others, and hold each other accountable. Discussing the material with others can deepen your understanding and provide new perspectives on applying the principles of Christlikeness in different contexts. Group activities and discussions can also foster a sense of camaraderie and mutual encouragement, helping you to stay motivated and committed to your spiritual journey.

AS WE EMBARK on this transformative journey together, may we be inspired by Jesus Christ's example and empowered by the guiding presence of the Holy Spirit. May this book catalyze personal growth, spiritual renewal, and a deeper connection to the source of all love and grace. Let us approach this journey with a spirit of openness and humility, ready to be transformed by the power of Christ's example.

REMEMBER that the journey toward Christlikeness is a lifelong process. It requires patience, perseverance, and a willingness to seek God's guidance and strength continually. There will be challenges and setbacks along the way, but with each step, you will grow closer to the ideal of Christlike living. Embrace this journey with hope and determination, knowing that as you strive to emulate Christ, you are participating in the divine work of bringing healing, hope, and love to the world.

. . .

"How to Be Christlike" is more than just a book; it is a guide and companion on your spiritual journey. Through thoughtful reflection, practical exercises, and the support of a faith community, you will be equipped to grow in Christlikeness and to make a positive impact in the world. May this book inspire you to live out the teachings of Jesus with authenticity and grace, and may you find joy and fulfillment in pursuing a Christlike life.

CHAPTER 2

THE ESSENCE OF CHRIST'S CHARACTER

The Core Attributes of Jesus

To understand the essence of Christ's character, it is essential to delve into the core attributes that define his life and ministry. These attributes are not just ideals to be admired from a distance; they are qualities that Jesus consistently demonstrated and called his followers to embody. The primary characteristics of Jesus include love, compassion, humility, integrity, forgiveness, and faith. Each attribute contributes to a holistic understanding of Christ's character and provides a model for how we can live our lives in alignment with his teachings.

Love

LOVE IS THE CORNERSTONE OF JESUS' character, the bedrock upon which his entire ministry rests, and the beacon that illuminates his teachings. Throughout the Gospels, Jesus tirelessly underscores the importance of love in our relationship with God and our interactions. In Matthew 22:37-39, Jesus encapsulates the essence of divine commandments, affirming that the most significant mandates are to love the Lord our God with unreserved devotion and to love our neighbors as ourselves. This divine injunction transcends mere sentimentality, calling for a love that encompasses the totality of our being—heart, soul, and mind.

AT THE HEART OF JESUS' teachings lies agape love, characterized by its selflessness, sacrificial nature, and unwavering commitment to the well-being of others. Unlike the eros of romantic love or the philia of friendship, agape love transcends human boundaries and extends to friends and foes alike. It is a love that seeks not its interests but the flourishing of others, even at significant personal cost.

. . .

THE PINNACLE of this agape love is found in Jesus' ultimate act of self-sacrifice on the cross. In John 15:13, Jesus declares, "Greater love has no one than this: to lay down one's life for one's friends." In the crucible of suffering and shame, Jesus exemplifies the depths of divine love—a love that knows no bounds and spares no expense. His willingness to endure the agony of crucifixion for the sake of humanity stands as the epitome of love in its purest form.

MOREOVER, JESUS' love is not passive but active, prompting him to heal the sick, feed the hungry, and comfort the brokenhearted. His ministry was a living testament to the transformative power of love as he reached out to the marginalized, embraced the outcasts, and offered hope to the despairing. In his parables and teachings, Jesus vividly portrays the radical nature of divine love—a love that challenges societal norms, breaks down barriers, and embraces all who seek its embrace.

IN ESSENCE, JESUS' command to love encapsulates the spirit of his entire ministry—a ministry characterized by compassion, mercy, and grace. As his followers, we are called to embody this same selfless love, extending grace to the undeserving, kindness to the hurting, and forgiveness to the repentant. In doing so, we witness the transformative power of love and participate in God's redemptive work in the world.

Compassion

JESUS' ministry is a testament to the profound depths of compassion embodied in his every word and deed. His heart was stirred with empathy at the sight of human suffering, and his response was always of active compassion. Whether encountering the sick, the hungry, or the grieving, Jesus' compassion knew no bounds.

IN HIS HEALING MINISTRY, Jesus demonstrated a divine compassion that transcended physical restoration. He not only cured diseases but restored dignity and hope to the afflicted. Through his touch, the blind received sight, the lame walked, and the lepers were cleansed. His miracles were not displays of power for power's sake but expressions of love and compassion for those in need.

MOREOVER, JESUS' compassion extended beyond physical ailments to encompass humanity's spiritual and emotional wounds. He offered forgiveness to the repentant, comfort to the sorrowful, and hope to the despairing. His parables, such as the prodigal son and the lost sheep, reveal the depth of his compassion for the broken and the lost, affirming God's boundless grace for all who seek redemption.

ONE OF THE most poignant expressions of Jesus' compassion is his interactions with the marginalized and outcasts of society. In a culture marked by social stratification and exclusion, Jesus broke down barriers and reached out to those deemed untouchable by societal norms. He dined with tax collectors and sinners, welcomed children into his presence, and offered solace to the oppressed and despised. His compassion knew no bounds, embracing all with grace and love.

THE GOSPEL ACCOUNTS depict Jesus as "moved with compassion" (Matthew 9:36, Mark 1:41), which encapsulates the depth of his empathy and concern for humanity. His compassion was not a fleeting emotion but a guiding principle that permeated every aspect of his ministry. It compelled him to action, prompting him to meet the needs of the marginalized, challenge injustice, and offer a message of hope to the brokenhearted.

As followers of Christ, we are called to emulate his example of compassion in our lives. We are called to see beyond outward appearances to every individual's inherent dignity and worth. Like Jesus, we are called to extend compassion to the marginalized, the oppressed, and the overlooked, embodying the love and grace of God in tangible ways. In doing so, we witness the transformative power of compassion and participate in God's redemptive work in the world.

Humility

Despite the holy nature of his divinity, Jesus chose to embody humility in every aspect of his earthly existence. He demonstrated a profound reverence for humanity and a radical inversion of societal norms. His humility was not merely a passive attribute but an active principle that permeated his teachings and actions, challenging conventional notions of greatness and power.

At the outset of his earthly journey, Jesus entered the world not in a palace or a grand estate but in a humble manger—a stark symbol of his identification with the lowly and marginalized. His birth in Bethlehem, announced by angels to shepherds in the fields, signaled a radical redefinition of power and privilege. In choosing to dwell among the humble, Jesus affirmed the inherent worth and dignity of every human being, regardless of status or station.

. . .

THROUGHOUT HIS MINISTRY, Jesus consistently modeled a life of service and selflessness, prioritizing the needs of others above his comfort and convenience. He healed the sick, fed the hungry, and ministered to the outcasts of society, embodying the essence of servant leadership. His actions spoke volumes, illustrating that true greatness is not measured by titles or accolades but by the willingness to stoop down and serve others.

ONE OF THE most poignant demonstrations of Jesus' humility is found in his act of washing the feet of his disciples. In a culture where foot-washing was reserved for the lowest of servants, Jesus assumed the role of a humble servant-leader, stooping down to perform this menial task. His actions were symbolic and a powerful lesson in humility and servant leadership (John 13:14-15). By washing his disciples' feet, Jesus taught that true greatness is found in acts of humble service, not in pursuing power or recognition.

IN HIS TEACHINGS, Jesus repeatedly emphasized the importance of humility as a foundational virtue in the Kingdom of God. He declared, "The greatest among you will be your servant. For those who exalt themselves will be humbled, and those who humble themselves will be exalted" (Matthew 23:11-12). These words are a timeless reminder that true greatness is not found in self-promotion or self-aggrandizement but in a posture of humility and service.

IN ESSENCE, JESUS' life was a living embodiment of humility—a radical departure from the values of the world and a profound revelation of the Kingdom of God. His example challenges us to embrace humility as a guiding principle in our own lives, to prioritize the needs of others, and to cultivate a spirit of servant leadership. In doing so, we follow in the footsteps of our humble Savior and bear witness to the transformative power of humility in building communities of grace and compassion.

Integrity

INTEGRITY WAS A HALLMARK OF JESUS' character. He lived a life of perfect moral uprightness, always aligning his actions with his teachings. Jesus condemned hypocrisy and called for genuine, heartfelt devotion to God (Matthew 23:27-28). His commitment to truth and righteousness remained steadfast, even in the face of persecution and death.

Forgiveness

FORGIVENESS IS CENTRAL TO JESUS' message. He taught his followers to forgive others as God has forgiven them (Matthew 6:14-15). On the cross, Jesus exemplified ultimate forgiveness, asking God to forgive those who crucified him (Luke 23:34). His teachings and actions underscore the transformative power of forgiveness in healing relationships and restoring communities.

Faith

JESUS' unwavering faith in God the Father was evident throughout his life. He trusted in God's plan and demonstrated reliance on prayer and divine guidance (Luke 5:16, John 5:19). Jesus encouraged his followers to have faith in God, assuring them that faith can move mountains and that nothing is impossible with God (Matthew 17:20, Mark 9:23).

Why These Attributes Matter

THE ATTRIBUTES of Jesus are not just abstract virtues; they are essential for living a life pleasing to God and impactful to others. Understanding why these attributes matter is crucial for appreciating their significance and striving to embody them daily.

Reflecting God's Love

BY EMBODYING JESUS' love, we reflect the nature of God, who is love (1 John 4:8). This love is transformative, fostering deeper connections with others and building a sense of community and belonging. It transcends race, religion, and social status barriers, promoting unity and peace. Living out this love in practical ways, such as showing kindness, offering support, and advocating for justice, allows us to be conduits of God's love in a broken world.

Promoting Healing and Compassion

AS JESUS EXEMPLIFIED, compassion encompasses a holistic approach to addressing individuals' physical, emotional, and spiritual needs. His life and ministry were marked by profound acts of kindness that transcended mere sympathy and moved toward active engagement in alleviating the suffering of others. By practicing compassion in our own lives, we become instruments of healing and channels of God's love and grace.

. . .

WHEN WE CARE for the sick, we mirror Jesus' numerous healings, where he restored health and dignity to those afflicted by illness. This act of compassion not only addresses physical ailments but also offers emotional support and spiritual reassurance, affirming the inherent worth of every person.

COMFORTING the grieving is another vital expression of compassion. Jesus wept with those who mourned, such as when he was deeply moved by Mary and Martha's sorrow over the death of their brother Lazarus. By offering a listening ear, a comforting presence, and empathetic support to those in sorrow, we help ease their pain and provide a sense of solace and hope amidst their grief.

THEY SUPPORT those distressed due to emotional turmoil, financial hardship, or social exclusion. This reflects the inclusive love of Jesus, who reached out to the marginalized and oppressed. Acts of compassion in these contexts can involve providing practical assistance, offering words of encouragement, and advocating for justice and equity.

WE EMBODY JESUS' healing ministry through these compassionate actions, bringing light and hope to those in need. Compassion becomes a tangible expression of our faith, allowing us to participate in God's redemptive work by promoting healing, fostering connection, and nurturing the well-being of our communities.

Cultivating Humility

HUMILITY IS vital for personal growth and relational harmony. It enables us to recognize our limitations, learn from others, and serve selflessly. By cultivating humility, we become more approachable, build stronger relationships, and foster a culture of respect and cooperation. Humility also guards against pride and self-right-eousness, helping us to stay grounded and focused on serving God and others.

Upholding Integrity

INTEGRITY FOSTERS TRUST AND CREDIBILITY. When our actions align with our beliefs, we build a reputation for reliability and honesty. This integrity is crucial in personal relationships, professional settings, and leadership roles. Upholding integrity means making ethical decisions, standing up for what is right, and living consistently with our values, even when challenging.

Embracing Forgiveness

FORGIVENESS IS a pillar of personal peace and relational harmony, offering liberation from bitterness and hatred. It is a transformative act that paves the way for reconciliation and healing within ourselves and our interactions with others. As Jesus exemplified through his teachings and actions, embracing forgiveness is not merely an option but a vital necessity for fostering emotional well-being and nurturing healthier, more compassionate relationships.

BY EXTENDING FORGIVENESS, we release ourselves from resentment and anger, allowing emotional freedom and inner peace to flourish. It empowers us to let go of past grievances and hurts, freeing up space for love, empathy, and understanding. Moreover, forgiveness creates a fertile ground for reconciliation, fostering the restoration of broken relationships and the rebuilding of trust.

FOLLOWING THE EXAMPLE OF JESUS, who offered forgiveness even from the cross, we learn to transcend our human inclination towards vengeance and retribution. Instead, we embrace a spirit of grace and mercy, recognizing our need for forgiveness and extending the same to others. This act of radical forgiveness reflects the boundless grace we have received from God and catalyzes a cycle of forgiveness and grace within our communities.

ULTIMATELY, forgiveness is a choice—a deliberate and courageous decision to let go of past hurts and embrace a future filled with hope and reconciliation. It requires humility, empathy, and a willingness to extend grace even to those who may not deserve it. Cultivating a culture of forgiveness in our personal lives and communities creates a more compassionate and empathetic world where healing and reconciliation can flourish.

Strengthening Faith

FAITH IS the bedrock upon which we build our lives, providing a steady foundation amid life's uncertainties and trials. It offers a sense of assurance and security, reminding us that we are not alone in our journey but are upheld by God's unwavering presence. Faith becomes our anchor in times of doubt and confusion, grounding us in the unchanging truth of God's promises.

· · ·

Moreover, faith empowers us to face challenges with courage and resilience. It instills a sense of inner strength and conviction, enabling us to confront adversity with confidence and perseverance. Instead of being overcome by fear or despair, we are encouraged to stand firm in our beliefs, knowing God is with us every step.

Cultivating faith involves continually surrendering our will to God's divine plan, trusting His ways are higher than ours. It requires a willingness to let go of our understanding and lean into God's wisdom and guidance. As we deepen our faith, we become more attuned to God's voice and receptive to His leadership.

Faith inspires us to boldly obey God's calling, even when the path ahead seems uncertain. It fuels our willingness to take risks and make sacrifices for the sake of His kingdom, knowing that He will equip and empower us for the task at hand. In this way, faith becomes a source of comfort, strength, and a catalyst for transformative action as we seek to live out God's purposes with confidence and conviction.

How to Reflect These Attributes in Daily Life

Reflecting Christ's attributes in daily life involves intentional actions, consistent practice, and reliance on divine guidance. Here are practical steps to help integrate these virtues into everyday interactions and decisions.

Practicing Love

1. Acts of Kindness: Perform random acts of kindness, such as helping a neighbor, volunteering, or offering a listening ear to someone in distress. Small gestures can make a significant impact.
2. Building Relationships: Invest time in building and nurturing relationships. Show genuine interest in others' lives, celebrate their joys, and support them in their struggles.
3. Advocating for Justice: Stand up for the marginalized and oppressed. Advocate for policies and practices that promote equality, justice, and dignity for all people.

Cultivating Compassion

1. Active Listening: Practice active listening and show empathy and understanding without judgment. This fosters a sense of being heard and valued.
2. Service: Engage in community service projects or charitable activities. Serving others helps to develop a compassionate heart and provides practical help to those in need.
3. Mindfulness: Be mindful of the needs around you. Small acts of compassion, such as offering help to a coworker or reaching out to a lonely friend, can make a big difference.

Embracing Humility

1. Serving Others: Look for opportunities to serve others without seeking recognition. Simple acts like helping with household chores or supporting a colleague can demonstrate humility.
2. Learning from Others: Be open to feedback and willing to learn from others. Recognize that everyone has something valuable to contribute.
3. Admitting Mistakes: When you make a mistake, acknowledge it and seek to make amends. This demonstrates humility and a commitment to personal growth.

Upholding Integrity

1. Honest Communication: Always speak the truth, even when it is difficult. Avoid exaggeration and be straightforward in your communications.
2. Ethical Decisions: Make decisions based on moral principles, even if they are unpopular or challenging. Stand by your convictions.
3. Consistency: Ensure that your actions consistently reflect your values. Live out your faith in all areas of life, not just in religious settings.

Practicing Forgiveness

1. Letting Go of Grudges: Make a conscious effort to overcome grudges and past hurts. Holding onto resentment harms you more than the other person.

2. Seeking Reconciliation: When conflicts arise, seek to resolve them through open, honest, and respectful dialogue. Be willing to forgive and ask for forgiveness.
3. Extending Grace: Offer grace to others, understanding that everyone makes mistakes. Treat others with the same forgiveness and compassion you have received from God.

Strengthening Faith

1. Prayer: Develop a regular prayer routine to communicate with God. Prayer strengthens your relationship with Him and provides guidance and comfort.
2. Bible Study: Engage in regular Bible study to deepen your understanding of God's word and His will for your life. Apply biblical principles to your daily decisions and actions.
3. Fellowship: Participate in a faith community where you can grow alongside others, share experiences, and support one another in your faith journeys.

INCORPORATING Jesus's core attributes into our daily lives requires intentionality, practice, and reliance on God's grace. Focusing on love, compassion, humility, integrity, forgiveness, and faith can reflect Christ's character and impact our world. These attributes guide our personal growth and enable us to provide hope, healing, and transformation in our communities. As we strive to emulate Christ, we bring God's love and grace to a needy world.

MICHAEL STEVENS

CHAPTER 3

FAITH AND DEVOTION

∼

Faith and devotion are central to Christlike living, providing both the foundation and the fuel for a life that reflects the teachings and example of Jesus. This chapter delves into the crucial role of faith, explores how to develop a devoted heart, and offers practical steps to strengthen one's faith.

. . .

The Role of Faith in Christlike Living

FAITH IS the foundation of the Christian experience, anchoring believers in their relationship with God and guiding them toward discipleship. At its essence, faith is the bridge that connects humanity with the divine, enabling individuals to receive the gift of salvation and embark on a transformative journey of spiritual growth.

CENTRAL to the Christian faith is accepting salvation through faith in Jesus Christ. Through faith, individuals acknowledge their need for redemption and trust in the finished work of Christ on the cross for the forgiveness of sins. This act of faith initiates a profound spiritual transformation, as believers are reconciled to God and adopted into His family as beloved children.

FAITH ALSO ENTAILS deep trust in God's promises, as Scripture reveals. Throughout the Bible, God makes numerous assurances to His people, promising never to leave nor forsake them, to provide for their needs, and to work together for their good. Believers find strength, comfort, and hope amid life's uncertainties by embracing these promises with unwavering confidence.

MOREOVER, faith relies on God's guidance and leadership in every aspect of life. By surrendering control and yielding to God's sovereignty, individuals allow Him to direct their steps, illuminate their paths, and orchestrate their circumstances according to His divine will. This reliance on God's guidance fosters a deep intimacy with the Creator and cultivates a sense of peace and security amidst life's storms.

FAITH IS NOT MERELY a passive belief or intellectual assent but an active, dynamic trust that permeates every facet of the believer's existence. Through faith, individuals receive salvation, embrace God's promises, and entrust their lives to His guiding hand. As the cornerstone of the Christian life, faith empowers believers to walk in obedience, experience divine transformation, and journey ever closer to God's heart.

Foundation of Relationship with God

FAITH IS how we enter into and maintain a relationship with God. We believe in Jesus Christ as our Savior through faith and receive the grace that leads to eternal life (Ephesians 2:8-9). Without faith, it is impossible to please God (Hebrews 11:6), for faith is the basis of our trust in His character and word.

THIS FOUNDATIONAL RELATIONSHIP is not static; it is dynamic and growing. Faith, like a living organism, must be nurtured and cultivated. Regular prayer, worship, and studying the Scriptures deepen our understanding of God and what He desires for our lives. This continuous growth in faith helps us to stay connected to God's will and aligned with His purposes.

Faith as a Guiding Principle

FAITH IS the guiding light that illuminates the believer's path, directing their decisions and actions in alignment with God's will. Faith provides a steadfast anchor in a world fraught with uncertainty and complexity, grounding individuals in a sense of purpose and direction.

AT ITS CORE, faith is a conscious choice to trust in God's wisdom and sovereignty, acknowledging His ultimate authority over all aspects of life. This trust empowers believers to navigate life's challenges confidently, knowing that God's plans are ultimately for their good (Jeremiah 29:11). By aligning their decisions with God's will, individuals ensure that their actions reflect His love, grace, and righteousness.

IN TIMES of adversity and indecision, faith is a compass, guiding believers towards paths that honor God's commands and character. This guiding principle is especially crucial amidst the myriad of conflicting values and temptations in today's world. Faith provides discernment, enabling individuals to distinguish between what is pleasing to God and what is not. With faith as their guide, believers can walk in integrity and righteousness, upholding the principles of truth and justice even in the face of opposition.

ULTIMATELY, faith empowers individuals to live with purpose and conviction, confident in their identity as children of God. It infuses their decisions and actions with meaning and significance, leading them to spiritual growth and transformation. As believers trust in God's guidance and surrender to His will, they find fulfillment in knowing that their lives are aligned with His divine purpose.

Source of Strength and Resilience

FAITH GIVES us the strength to endure hardships and persevere through trials. It reassures us of God's presence and His promise to work all things for our good (Romans 8:28). This resilience, born of faith, allows us to face adversity with hope and confidence, knowing that our lives are in God's hands.

THE BIBLE IS replete with stories of individuals whose faith enabled them to overcome immense challenges. From Abraham's faith in God's promises to Daniel's trust in God's protection, these examples inspire us to hold fast to our faith regardless of circumstances. In our own lives, faith helps us to see beyond our immediate struggles and trust in God's overarching plan.

Faith in Community

OUR FAITH FINDS fertile ground to flourish and thrive within the community of believers. The church, often called the body of Christ, is a nurturing environment where individuals can find support, encouragement, and accountability in their spiritual journey.

ONE OF THE church's primary functions is to provide believers with a sense of belonging and community. Through shared worship, study, and fellowship, church family members come together to edify one another and grow in spiritual maturity. This collective experience fosters a sense of unity and solidarity among believers, strengthening their bond as members of the body of Christ.

. . .

BEING part of a faith community offers numerous benefits for individual believers. It provides a safe space to share joys and burdens with others who understand and empathize with their experiences. In times of trial or celebration, believers can lean on their church family for support and encouragement, finding solace in knowing they are not alone in their journey.

COLLECTIVE WORSHIP within the faith community is a powerful catalyst for spiritual growth. As believers gather together to lift their voices in praise and adoration, their faith is uplifted and enriched by the collective experience of God's presence. Through hymns, prayers, and Scripture readings, believers are reminded of God's faithfulness and goodness, deepening their trust and reliance on Him.

FURTHERMORE, the diversity within the faith community offers a rich tapestry of perspectives and insights that contribute to the collective understanding of God's word and ways. Believers from different backgrounds and walks of life bring unique experiences and interpretations to the table, enriching the communal study of Scripture and fostering a deeper appreciation for the multifaceted nature of God's truth.

IN SUMMARY, the church is vital in nurturing and strengthening our faith. It provides a supportive community where believers can find encouragement, accountability, and spiritual growth. Through shared worship, study, and fellowship, believers are equipped to navigate the ups and downs of life's journey with faith and resilience.

Developing a Devoted Heart

DEVOTION IS the natural outpouring of faith, representing a profound and heartfelt commitment to God and His divine purposes. It encompasses a deep-seated love for God, a genuine desire to please Him, and a wholehearted willingness to surrender one's life to His service.

AT THE CORE of devotion lies a profound love for God—transcending mere emotion and permeating every aspect of one's being. This love is rooted in an intimate relationship with the Creator, nurtured through prayer, worship, and communion with Him. It acknowledges God's unfailing goodness, faithfulness, and grace, prompting an unreserved affection and devotion.

DEVOTION IS ALSO CHARACTERIZED by a sincere desire to please God. It involves aligning one's thoughts, words, and actions with His will to honor and glorify Him in every aspect of life. This desire for divine approval springs from a deep reverence for God's holiness and a recognition of His sovereign authority over all creation.

FURTHERMORE, devotion entails surrendering one's life entirely to God's service. It is a relinquishment of self-will and personal ambitions in favor of God's purposes and plans. This surrender is not a passive resignation but an active choice to yield to God's leading, trusting in His wisdom and guidance for the future.

DEVOTION IS NOT MERELY a fleeting sentiment but a steadfast commitment that perseveres through trials and challenges. It is a lifelong journey of growth and transformation, marked by an unwavering dedication to God and His kingdom. As believers cultivate a devoted heart, they experience the fullness of joy and fulfillment that comes from living in intimate communion with their Creator.

Cultivating Love for God

LOVE FOR GOD is the primary motivation for devotion. This love is nurtured through regular prayer, worship, and meditation on God's word. As we spend time in His presence, we grow in understanding His love for us, deepening our love for Him (1 John 4:19).

OUR LOVE for God is also expressed through obedience to His commands. Jesus said, "If you love me, keep my commands" (John 14:15). This obedience is not born out of obligation but a genuine desire to honor and please the One who loves us unconditionally.

Obedience and Surrender

A DEVOTED HEART is marked by obedience to God's commands and a willingness to surrender our will to His. Jesus modeled perfect obedience, submitting to the Father's will even unto death (Philippians 2:8). Following His example demonstrates our devotion and commitment to God's purposes.

SURRENDER INVOLVES LETTING GO of our desires and plans in favor of God's will. This can be challenging, as it requires us to trust that God's plans are better than our own. However, surrendering to

God's will brings peace and fulfillment, as we know that we live in alignment with His perfect plan for our lives.

Pursuing Holiness

DEVOTION TO GOD entails a steadfast commitment to holiness—a dedication to living a life set apart for His purposes. This pursuit of holiness is not a one-time event but an ongoing process of sanctification, empowered by the indwelling presence of the Holy Spirit.

HOLINESS, in essence, involves a separation from the patterns of this world and a consecration to God's divine will. It requires vigilance in guarding our hearts and minds against the influences of sin and worldliness and a deliberate effort to align our thoughts, words, and actions with God's standards of righteousness.

HOWEVER, holiness is not synonymous with perfection. Instead, it is about striving for excellence in character and conduct, acknowledging our human frailty while relying on God's grace for transformation. It is a journey of growth and refinement, marked by a continual surrender to the sanctifying work of the Holy Spirit in our lives.

LIVING a holy life entails making daily decisions to prioritize God's kingdom values over this world's fleeting pleasures and pursuits. It involves cultivating virtues such as love, humility, integrity, and compassion, which reflect Christ's character and serve as a beacon of light in a darkened world.

. . .

BY PURSUING HOLINESS, we become vessels through which God's love and grace can flow to others. Our lives become living testimonies of God's transforming power, drawing others into a relationship with Him and pointing them toward the abundant life in Christ.

IN SUMMARY, devotion to God necessitates a commitment to holiness —a daily striving to live according to His will and reflect His character in all we do. Through the ongoing process of sanctification, empowered by the Holy Spirit, we become vessels through which God's love and grace can transform lives and bring glory to His name.

Service to Others

TRUE DEVOTION IS EXPRESSED in service to others. Jesus taught that loving God and loving others are inseparable (Matthew 22:37-40). Our dedication to God is reflected in acts of kindness, compassion, and justice toward our neighbors. By serving others, we serve God and fulfill His command to love one another.

SERVICE TO OTHERS also deepens our faith and devotion, allowing us to experience God's love tangibly. When we serve, we become conduits of God's grace and blessings and grow in understanding His love and compassion for all people.

Practical Steps to Strengthen Faith

STRENGTHENING faith requires intentional effort and discipline. Here are practical steps to help cultivate and deepen your faith:

. . .

Daily Prayer and Meditation

CONSISTENT DAILY PRAYER and meditation on Scripture are essential for nurturing faith. Set aside time daily to communicate with God, seek His guidance, and reflect on His word. This practice builds a strong foundation for your faith and keeps you connected to God's presence.

IN ADDITION TO TRADITIONAL PRAYER, consider incorporating practices such as lectio divina, a method of meditative scripture reading, or the examen, a reflective prayer practice that helps you discern God's presence in your daily life.

Regular Worship and Fellowship

PARTICIPATE REGULARLY in corporate worship and fellowship with other believers. Engaging in communal worship, studying the Bible, and sharing in the sacraments strengthen your faith and provide mutual encouragement and support.

WORSHIP IS NOT JUST about singing songs or attending church services; it's about experiencing God's presence and responding to His greatness. Regular fellowship with other believers helps keep you accountable and provides a support network as you grow in your faith.

Study of Scripture

DEEPEN your understanding of God's word through regular and systematic study of the Bible. Use study guides, commentaries, and other resources to gain insight into the Scriptures. Memorize key verses that speak to your heart and reinforce your faith.

CONSIDER JOINING or forming a Bible study group where you can discuss and reflect on Scripture with others. This communal approach can provide deeper insights and foster a greater sense of connection to the biblical text.

Acts of Service and Charity

PUT your faith into action through acts of service and charity. Volunteering, helping those in need, and engaging in social justice initiatives are tangible expressions of your faith and devotion. Serving others benefits them and strengthens your faith as you see God working through you.

LOOK for opportunities to serve within your church and community. Whether participating in a food drive, visiting the sick, or mentoring youth, acts of service help embody the love of Christ and positively impact those around you.

Seek Spiritual Mentorship

FIND a mentor or spiritual advisor who can guide your faith journey. Someone with more experience can offer valuable insights, encouragement, and accountability. Engaging in discipleship relationships helps you to grow and mature in your faith.

. . .

MENTORSHIP CAN TAKE MANY FORMS, from formal spiritual direction to informal conversations with a trusted friend. The key is to find someone who can offer wisdom and support as you navigate your spiritual journey.

Cultivate Gratitude and Contentment

PRACTICE GRATITUDE BY REGULARLY REFLECTING on God's blessings in your life. Keeping a gratitude journal can help you focus on the positive aspects of your faith journey. Cultivating contentment allows you to trust God's provision and timing, reinforcing your faith in His goodness.

GRATITUDE SHIFTS your focus from what you lack to what you have, fostering a sense of contentment and peace. Regularly giving thanks develops a more positive and hopeful outlook, strengthening your faith.

Embrace Challenges as Opportunities for Growth

VIEW TRIALS and challenges as opportunities to deepen your faith. Instead of being discouraged, seek to understand what God may be teaching you through difficult circumstances. Persevere in faith, trusting that God is refining and strengthening you through every trial.

. . .

DIFFICULTIES OFTEN PROVIDE the most significant opportunities for spiritual growth. They teach us to rely more fully on God and trust His wisdom and timing. By embracing challenges positively, you can grow stronger in your faith and more resilient in your spiritual journey.

Engage in Spiritual Disciplines

INCORPORATE VARIOUS SPIRITUAL disciplines into your routine, such as fasting, solitude, and contemplative prayer. These practices help to deepen your relationship with God, enhance your spiritual awareness, and strengthen your faith.

SPIRITUAL DISCIPLINES ARE tools that help you to focus your heart and mind on God. They create space for you to listen to His voice and experience His presence more profoundly. By regularly practicing these disciplines, you cultivate a more vibrant and dynamic faith.

Share Your Faith

SHARE your faith with others through personal testimony, evangelism, and discipleship. Talking about your faith reinforces your beliefs and helps spread Jesus's message. It also encourages you to live out your faith more authentically.

SHARING your faith can take many forms, from casual conversations with friends to more formal evangelistic efforts. The important thing is to be open and willing to speak about your relationship with God and the impact of faith in your life. Doing so strengthens your faith and invites others to experience the transformative power of a relationship with Christ.

Reflect and Renew

TAKE time to reflect on your spiritual journey and assess your growth in faith. Periodically evaluate your practices, commitments, and areas for development. Seek renewal through retreats, spiritual workshops, and dedicated times of solitude and prayer.

REFLECTION HELPS you to stay aware of your spiritual progress and to identify areas where you may need to make adjustments. It also provides opportunities for renewal and rejuvenation, allowing you to refocus your efforts and deepen your commitment to your faith journey.

FAITH AND DEVOTION are integral to living a Christlike life. By understanding the role of religion, developing a devoted heart, and taking practical steps to strengthen your faith, you can grow closer to God and reflect His character in your daily life. This journey of faith is ongoing, requiring continuous effort and commitment. However, the rewards are immeasurable as you experience the fullness of life in Christ and become a source of hope and transformation in the world.

CHAPTER 4
LOVE AND COMPASSION

Understanding Christ's Love

A t the heart of Christianity lies the profound and transformative concept of love, exemplified in the life and teachings of Jesus Christ. Understanding Christ's love requires delving into His sacrificial nature, boundless compassion, and unwavering commitment to humanity.

CHRIST'S LOVE, often called agape love, is characterized by its selfless and unconditional nature. Unlike human love, which is usually conditional and based on merit, Christ's love knows no bounds or limitations. It is a love that seeks the highest good for others, even at significant personal cost.

CENTRAL TO UNDERSTANDING Christ's love is the recognition of His sacrificial death on the cross. Jesus willingly laid down His life as a demonstration of His love for humanity, bearing the weight of sin and offering redemption to all who would believe in Him. His ultimate act of selflessness is the epitome of love, inspiring believers to emulate His example in their own lives.

FURTHERMORE, Christ's love is marked by His boundless compassion towards the marginalized, the outcast, and the oppressed. Throughout His ministry, Jesus demonstrated a deep empathy for the suffering and a willingness to extend grace and mercy to those in need. His compassionate deeds, whether healing the sick, feeding the hungry, or comforting the grieving, reveal the depth of His love for humanity.

Cultivating Compassion for Others

AS RECIPIENTS of Christ's love, believers are called to cultivate compassion for others, following in the footsteps of their Savior. Compassion involves not only feeling empathy towards those who are suffering but also taking action to alleviate their pain and meet their needs. One of the critical aspects of cultivating compassion is developing a heart that is attuned to the needs of others. This requires practicing empathy—putting ourselves in the shoes of hurting people and seeking to understand their experiences and emotions. By empathizing with others, we open ourselves to their pain and create a space for genuine connection and healing.

CULTIVATING compassion is a transformative journey that begins with self-awareness and extends outward to encompass the needs of others. It requires a willingness to step outside of our own experiences and perspectives and enter into the lived realities of those around us. In doing so, we acknowledge every individual's inherent worth and dignity and recognize our interconnectedness as members of the human family.

AT THE HEART of compassion is empathy, the ability to understand and share another person's feelings. Empathy enables us to bridge the gap between ourselves and others, forging connections based on mutual understanding and respect. It allows us to see beyond surface-level differences and recognize the common humanity that binds us.

PRACTICING empathy involves active listening and genuine engagement with the experiences of others. It requires setting aside preconceived notions and biases and approaching each interaction with an open mind and a compassionate heart. By listening attentively to the stories and struggles of others, we validate their experiences and affirm their worth as individuals created in the image of God.

EMPATHY ALSO INVOLVES the willingness to bear witness to the pain and suffering of others without turning away. It requires a willingness to sit with discomfort and uncertainty, knowing that our presence alone can provide comfort and solace to those in need. By offering a compassionate presence, we communicate to others that they are not alone in their struggles and that their pain is seen and acknowledged.

CULTIVATING compassion requires empathy and a commitment to action. It is not enough to feel sympathy for those suffering; we must actively seek ways to alleviate their pain and meet their needs. This may involve tangible acts of service, such as providing food, shelter, or clothing to those in need or offering emotional support and encouragement to those struggling.

COMPASSIONATE ACTION also extends to advocating for systemic change and social justice. It requires a willingness to confront injustice and inequality wherever it may be found and to work towards creating a more just and equitable society for all. This may involve challenging oppressive systems and structures, amplifying the voices of marginalized communities, and advocating for policies that promote the common good.

CULTIVATING compassion is a lifelong journey that requires intentionality, humility, and a willingness to learn and grow. It is rooted in Christ's love and guided by His example of selfless service and sacrificial love. As we strive to cultivate compassion, may the Holy Spirit empower us to be agents of healing, reconciliation, and hope in a world in need.

Practical Ways to Show Love and Compassion

PRACTICING love and compassion is a tangible expression of Christ's love in action. It involves stepping out of our comfort zones, reaching out to those in need, and meeting them where they are. There are countless ways to demonstrate love and compassion, ranging from simple acts of kindness to more significant gestures of generosity and service.

RECOGNIZING every individual's inherent dignity and worth is at the heart of showing love and compassion. Every person is created in the image of God and deserving of love, respect, and compassion. By extending love and kindness to others, we reflect Christ's love and participate in the ongoing work of God's kingdom on earth.

ONE OF THE simplest yet most profound ways to show love and compassion is through acts of kindness. These acts can take many forms, from offering a smile and a word of encouragement to holding the door open for someone or helping a stranger in need. Small gestures of kindness may seem insignificant, but they can brighten someone's day and lift their spirits.

ANOTHER WAY TO demonstrate love and compassion is by actively listening to others and offering a compassionate presence. Listening attentively to someone can profoundly express care and compassion in a world of distractions and noise. By giving someone our full attention and being fully present in the moment, we communicate that their thoughts, feelings, and experiences matter.

ACTS OF SERVICE are another powerful way to show love and compassion in action. We may volunteer our time and talents to serve those in need through community organizations, charitable ministries, or church outreach programs. Whether we serve meals at a homeless shelter, tutor underprivileged children, or visit older people in nursing homes, acts of service provide tangible assistance and support to those who need it most.

GENEROSITY IS ALSO an essential aspect of demonstrating love and compassion. This may involve sharing our resources with those who are less fortunate, whether through financial donations, material goods, or other forms of assistance. Generosity enables us to meet the practical needs of others and alleviate their suffering, demonstrating Christ's love in a tangible and meaningful way.

IN ADDITION to these individual acts of kindness, there are opportunities to show love and compassion on a larger scale through advocacy and activism. This may involve speaking out against injustice and oppression, advocating for the rights of the marginalized and vulnerable, and working towards systemic change in our communities and society. By raising awareness of social issues and advocating for policies promoting justice and equality, we can create a more compassionate and inclusive world for all.

. . .

ULTIMATELY, showing love and compassion is not just about what we do but also the attitude and intention behind our actions. It is about approaching others with humility, empathy, and a genuine desire to alleviate their suffering and bring comfort and hope into their lives. As followers of Christ, may we be known not only for our words but also for our deeds as we seek to love and serve others in the same way that Christ has loved and served us?

Some practical ways to show love and compassion include:

ACTS OF KINDNESS:

Acts of kindness serve as the gentle whispers of compassion in a noisy world, offering solace and support to those in need. Whether lending a compassionate ear to someone's troubles, offering sincere encouragement, or performing unexpected acts of kindness, these small gestures carry immeasurable weight in brightening someone's day and embodying Christ's love in action.

BY OFFERING A LISTENING EAR, we create a sanctuary for others to share their burdens and find comfort in knowing they are heard and understood. Likewise, genuine encouragement can uplift spirits and infuse hope into weary hearts. Through random acts of kindness, we extend the hand of fellowship and demonstrate solidarity with our fellow human beings, reminding them of their inherent worth and dignity in the eyes of God. Though small in scale, these acts can ignite a chain reaction of compassion and kindness, illuminating the world with the transformative power of Christ's love.

. . .

SERVICE TO OTHERS:

Volunteering time and resources to serve those in need is a tangible manifestation of love and compassion. Whether through community outreach programs, engagement with charitable organizations, or participation in church ministries, the impact of such contributions cannot be overstated.

BY VOLUNTEERING, individuals actively engage with the needs of their communities, demonstrating a commitment to making a positive difference in the lives of others. This hands-on approach allows volunteers to address pressing social issues, from homelessness and hunger to education and healthcare disparities.

MOREOVER, volunteering fosters a sense of connection and solidarity among participants as they work together to serve the marginalized or disadvantaged. Volunteers meet immediate needs and cultivate a culture of compassion and empathy through their collective efforts, laying the groundwork for lasting change and transformation within their communities.

SHARING RESOURCES:

Sharing material resources with those who are less fortunate is a tangible demonstration of Christ's love and provision in action. Whether providing food to the hungry, clothing to the needy, or financial assistance to those facing hardship, these acts of generosity reflect Christ's selfless and compassionate nature.

IN EXTENDING SUCH ASSISTANCE, individuals acknowledge every person's inherent dignity and worth, recognizing their shared humanity and interconnectedness. By meeting the practical needs of others, whether through direct donations or support to charitable organizations, individuals offer tangible relief and a message of hope and solidarity.

FURTHERMORE, sharing material resources fosters community and mutual support as individuals come together to address their neighbors' challenges. It reminds us that we are called to be stewards of God's blessings, sharing generously with others and trusting in His provision to meet our needs. Through such acts of generosity, individuals embody Christ's love and His command to love our neighbors as ourselves.

EXTENDING FORGIVENESS:

Choosing to forgive those who have wronged us, mirroring Christ's forgiveness towards us, is a profoundly impactful act of love and compassion. It is a conscious decision to release resentment and bitterness, paving the way for reconciliation and healing.

FORGIVENESS ACKNOWLEDGES the humanity in both the offender and the offended, recognizing that we are all flawed and need grace. Individuals demonstrate empathy and understanding by extending forgiveness and prioritizing restoration over retaliation.

MOREOVER, forgiveness liberates us from the burden of carrying grudges and past hurts, offering freedom and peace to both parties. It is a transformative process that allows for emotional healing and growth, fostering deeper connections and a culture of reconciliation.

. . .

ULTIMATELY, choosing to forgive reflects the transformative power of Christ's love in our lives as we emulate His example of grace and mercy toward others. It is a testament to love's redemptive nature and compassion's healing power in our relationships.

UNDERSTANDING CHRIST'S love and cultivating compassion for others are central tenets of the Christian faith. By following the example of Jesus Christ and actively seeking to demonstrate love and compassion in our daily lives, believers can become agents of transformation in a world in need of Christ's redeeming love.

CHAPTER 5
BOOK REVIEW REQUEST

Make a Difference with Your Review

Unlock the Power of Generosity

"Giving is not just about donating. It is about making a difference." - Kathy Calvin.

∿

DEAR READER,

Thank you for choosing "How to Be Christlike: A Journey of Faith, Transformation, and Legacy" by Michael Stevens. This book has guided you on your path of faith and inspired you to grow closer to Christ.

Why Your Review Matters

YOUR FEEDBACK IS CRITICAL. By sharing your thoughts on this book, you're helping others decide if it's the right resource for them and contributing to a broader conversation about faith and transformation.

How to Leave a Review

WRITING a review doesn't have to be complicated. Here are some simple steps to guide you:

1. Click **the Book's Review Link:** https://www.amazon.com/review/create-review/?ie=UTF8&channel=glance-detail&asin=B0D5HBFQG8

. . .

2. Scan the QR Code:

What to Include in Your Review

- **Personal Experience:** How did the book help you? Share specific examples.
- **Favorite Sections:** Highlight the parts of the book that were most beneficial.
- **Practical Impact:** Describe how you've applied the lessons and the changes you've seen.
- **Recommendation:** Would you recommend this book to others? Why or why not?

Example Review

"I FOUND 'HOW TO BE CHRISTLIKE' to be incredibly inspiring. The chapter on embracing forgiveness was a turning point for me. I've found a new sense of peace and connection with others by learning to forgive. The practical advice and heartfelt stories significantly impacted my faith journey. I highly recommend this book to anyone looking to deepen their relationship with Christ."

Your Impact

BY LEAVING A REVIEW, you're making a difference. Your insights can help others find spiritual guidance and encourage more open discussions about faith and personal transformation.

THANK you for taking the time to share your experience. Your voice matters; your review can help others on their faith journey.

WITH GRATITUDE,

MICHAEL Stevens

∿

CHAPTER 6

HUMILITY AND SERVANTHOOD

In a society that frequently idolizes self-promotion, personal achievement, and ambition, the virtues of humility and servanthood stand in stark contrast. These qualities are often viewed as signs of weakness or passivity in a culture that values assertiveness and self-confidence. However, in the context of Christlike living, humility and servanthood are not only fundamental but also transformative virtues that define the essence of true discipleship.

The Countercultural Nature of Humility and Servanthood

AT THE HEART of Christlike living is the call to adopt a posture of humility and a heart of servanthood. Unlike the world's standards, which often equate success with power, prestige, and recognition, the teachings of Jesus Christ turn these values upside down. Jesus proclaimed that "the greatest among you will be your servant" (Matthew 23:11), a radical redefinition of greatness that prioritizes service over status.

IN THE BIBLICAL SENSE, humility is not about devaluing oneself or engaging in false modesty. Instead, it involves a realistic assessment of oneself, recognizing one's strengths and weaknesses, and placing others' needs above one's own. It is about understanding our dependence on God and our interdependence with others, fostering a spirit of collaboration and mutual respect.

SERVANTHOOD, closely linked with humility, is about adopting an attitude of genuine care and concern for others. It is about being willing to serve, regardless of the task or the recognition it brings. Servanthood is rooted in love and compassion, driving us to meet the needs of those around us and to uplift the marginalized and the downtrodden.

The Profound Significance of Humility and Servanthood

THE VIRTUES of humility and servanthood are not mere moral ideals; they are central to the Christian faith and the life of discipleship. They are significant for several reasons:

REFLECTION OF CHRIST'S CHARACTER: Jesus Christ is the ultimate model of humility and servanthood. His incarnation—God becoming human—was an act of profound humility. Throughout His ministry, Jesus demonstrated these virtues in His interactions, teachings, and ultimately, in His sacrificial death on the cross. We reflect Christ's character to the world by embracing humility and servanthood.

SPIRITUAL GROWTH: Humility and servanthood are pathways to spiritual growth. They help us to develop a deeper relationship with God by fostering dependence on Him and a greater awareness of His grace. These virtues also cultivate a heart that is open to God's leading and responsive to the needs of others.

COMMUNITY BUILDING: In the Christian community, humility and servanthood are essential for building healthy, loving, and supportive relationships. They promote unity and cooperation, allowing us to work together for the common good. By serving one another, we create an environment where everyone feels valued and loved.

WITNESS TO THE WORLD: In a world that often prioritizes self-interest, humility and servanthood serve as powerful testimonies to the gospel's transformative power. When we live out these virtues, we witness the radical love of Jesus Christ, drawing others to Him through our example.

Embodying Humility and Servanthood: Lessons from Jesus Christ

JESUS CHRIST EMBODIED humility and servanthood in every aspect of His life and ministry. His birth in a humble manger, His life of simplicity, and His willingness to associate with the lowly and the outcast all point to His profound humility. Perhaps the most striking demonstration of His servant-heartedness was when He washed His disciples' feet—a task typically reserved for the lowest servant in the household (John 13:1-17). This act was a powerful symbol of His love and call for His followers to serve one another.

THROUGHOUT HIS MINISTRY, Jesus consistently taught and modeled these virtues. He encouraged His disciples to seek greatness through service, to love their neighbors as themselves, and to prioritize the needs of others. His parables, such as the Good Samaritan (Luke 10:25-37), illustrated the importance of compassion and selfless service.

The Transformative Power of Humility and Servanthood

THE VIRTUES of humility and servanthood can transform our lives and our world. By embracing these qualities, we undergo a fundamental shift in our perspective and our approach to life.

. . .

PERSONAL TRANSFORMATION: Humility and servanthood transform us from the inside out. They help us to overcome pride, selfishness, and the desire for recognition. Instead, we become more like Christ, characterized by love, compassion, and a willingness to serve. This transformation creates a more profound sense of peace, fulfillment, and purpose.

RELATIONAL TRANSFORMATION: Humility and servanthood transform our relationships. These virtues foster trust, respect, and mutual care, strengthening our bonds with others. They enable us to build communities marked by love and unity, where everyone is valued and supported.

SOCIETAL TRANSFORMATION: On a broader scale, humility and servanthood have the potential to bring about significant societal change. They challenge the status quo of power dynamics and social hierarchies, promoting justice, equality, and the common good. By serving others, especially the marginalized and the oppressed, we contribute to a more just and compassionate society.

Practical Steps to Cultivate Humility and Servanthood

TO CULTIVATE HUMILITY AND SERVANTHOOD, we must be intentional and proactive. Here are some practical steps to help us develop these virtues:

SELF-REFLECTION: Regularly examine your heart and motives. Does a desire for recognition drive your actions, or are they motivated by genuine love and service? Ask God to reveal areas of pride and self-centeredness and to help you cultivate a humble heart.

SERVICE: Look for opportunities to serve others in your daily life. Whether through acts of kindness, volunteering, or supporting those in need, make service a regular part of your routine. Remember that no act of service is too small or insignificant.

LISTENING AND LEARNING: Practice active listening and seek to understand the experiences and perspectives of others. Be open to learning from those around you, recognizing that everyone has something valuable to contribute.

GRATITUDE: Cultivate a spirit of gratitude for the gifts and opportunities God has given you. A grateful heart is a humble heart that acknowledges that everything we have is a gift from God.

PRAYER: Regularly pray for a heart of humility and a servant's spirit. Ask God to help you see others through His eyes and to give you the strength and willingness to serve.

BY EMBRACING HUMILITY AND SERVANTHOOD, we reflect Christ's character and experience the joy and fulfillment of living a life of love and service. These virtues transform our hearts, relationships, and world, drawing us closer to God and one another.

The Humility of Christ

AT THE HEART of Christ's ministry lay a radical humility that defied societal norms and expectations. Despite being the divine Son of God, Jesus chose humility as the cornerstone of His earthly mission. This humility was not a sign of weakness but strength, as Jesus willingly emptied Himself and took the form of a servant (Philippians 2:5-8). His entire life was a testament to humility, from His humble birth in a manger to His ultimate sacrifice on the cross.

JESUS' choice of humility began with His incarnation. The Creator of the universe, who held all power and glory, chose to be born in a lowly stable, wrapped in swaddling clothes, and laid in a manger (Luke 2:7). This birth was not in a palace or a place of honor but in the humblest of circumstances, accessible to shepherds and the poor. This act set the tone for Jesus' ministry and life—a life characterized by humility and service.

THROUGHOUT HIS EARTHLY MINISTRY, Jesus consistently modeled humility in His interactions with others. He welcomed the marginalized, dined with sinners, and showed compassion to society's outcasts. Jesus' humility was evident in His choice of companions and those He served. He did not seek the company of the rich and powerful; instead, He reached out to the lepers, the blind, the tax collectors, and the prostitutes—those whom society had rejected and scorned.

ONE SIGNIFICANT EXAMPLE OF JESUS' humility was His interaction with the Samaritan woman at the well (John 4:1-26). Jews typically avoided Samaritans, considering them unclean and inferior. Yet, Jesus spoke with her and revealed His identity as the Messiah to her. By doing so, He broke societal norms and demonstrated that God's love and salvation were available to all, regardless of social standing or past sins.

PERHAPS THE MOST poignant display of His humility was when He washed His disciples' feet—an act reserved for the lowliest servants (John 13:1-17). In doing so, Jesus demonstrated that true greatness is found in serving others and humbling oneself before God and one another. This act was revolutionary because it flipped the cultural expectations of leadership and greatness. Leaders were expected to be served, not to serve. Yet, Jesus, their Teacher and Lord, performed this menial task to teach them about servant leadership.

JESUS' humility was also evident in how He handled opposition and suffering. When He was arrested, mocked, and crucified, He did not retaliate or call down legions of angels to defend Him. Instead, He remained silent before His accusers and prayed for their forgiveness (Luke 23:34). This humility in the face of suffering is a powerful example for His followers. It teaches us that true strength lies not in asserting power over others but in enduring hardship with grace and forgiveness.

MOREOVER, JESUS' humility extended to His dependence on God the Father. Throughout His ministry, Jesus often withdrew to solitary places to pray (Mark 1:35, Luke 5:16). This reliance on prayer highlighted His dependence on the Father and His desire to align His will with God's will. Even in the Garden of Gethsemane, facing the agony of the cross, Jesus prayed, "Not my will, but yours be done" (Luke 22:42). This ultimate act of submission and trust exemplifies the depth of Jesus' humility and obedience.

. . .

IN ADDITION TO HIS ACTIONS, JESUS' teachings consistently emphasized humility. In the Beatitudes, He proclaimed, "Blessed are the poor in spirit, for theirs is the kingdom of heaven" (Matthew 5:3). He taught that those who humble themselves would be exalted (Matthew 23:12) and that the greatest in the kingdom of heaven are those who become like little children—innocent, trusting, and humble (Matthew 18:4). These teachings were countercultural and challenged the pride and self-reliance that were prevalent in society.

JESUS' parables also reinforced the importance of humility. The Parable of the Pharisee and the Tax Collector (Luke 18:9-14) contrasts the Pharisee's self-righteousness with the tax collector's humility, who acknowledged his sins and sought God's mercy. The tax collector, not the Pharisee, went home justified before God. This parable illustrates that God values a humble heart that recognizes its need for His grace over a proud heart that relies on its right-eousness.

THE APOSTLE PAUL encapsulated Christ's humility in his letter to the Philippians, urging believers to have the same mindset as Christ Jesus, who "made himself nothing by taking the very nature of a servant" (Philippians 2:7). Paul's exhortation is a call to believers to adopt a similar posture of humility and service in their own lives. They honor Christ and foster unity and love within the Christian community.

. . .

EMULATING Christ's humility involves a conscious decision to put others' needs above our own rather than to be served and to seek God's will above our desires. It means recognizing our limitations and dependence on God, being willing to learn from others, and showing grace and forgiveness even when wronged. This humility transforms relationships, communities, and, ultimately, the world.

LIVING out humility in today's world requires a countercultural mindset. It involves resisting the urge to seek recognition, power, and status, instead finding joy in serving others and elevating them. It calls for a willingness to listen, empathize, and act compassionately and kindly. Humility, as modeled by Christ, is not about thinking less of ourselves but of ourselves less, prioritizing the well-being and growth of others.

CHRIST'S HUMILITY is a profound and essential aspect of His character and ministry. His life, from His birth to His crucifixion, exemplifies a humility that defies societal expectations and reveals the heart of God. As His followers, we are called to embody this humility in our own lives, serving others selflessly, depending on God entirely, and living in a way that reflects the love and grace of Jesus. By doing so, we participate in the transformative work of God's kingdom, bringing hope, healing, and reconciliation to a world in desperate need of His love.

Embracing a Servant's Heart

CENTRAL to the concept of humility is the idea of servanthood—a willingness to serve others with humility and grace. Jesus exemplified this servant-heartedness, teaching His disciples that the greatest among them would be who served (Matthew 20:26-28). He called His followers to adopt a mindset of servanthood, encouraging them to prioritize the needs of others above their own.

EMBRACING a servant's heart requires a radical shift in perspective— a turning away from self-centeredness and a turning toward selflessness. It involves cultivating a deep compassion and empathy for others, recognizing their inherent dignity and worth as fellow image-bearers of God. It means putting aside our ambitions and agendas to uplift and empower those around us.

THIS CALL to servanthood is illustrated vividly in Jesus's life and teachings. In a society that often values power, status, and personal achievement, Jesus presented a revolutionary model of leadership and greatness. His approach was not to dominate or lord over others but to serve and elevate them. This fundamental principle of servanthood is encapsulated in His words: "The Son of Man did not come to be served, but to serve, and to give his life as a ransom for many" (Matthew 20:28).

ONE OF THE most potent examples of Jesus' servanthood is John 13, where He washes His disciples' feet. Traditionally performed by the lowest servant, this act was a shocking and profound demonstration of humility and love. By washing His disciples' feet, Jesus provided a practical service and set a profound example of servant leadership. He taught that no task should be beneath His followers if it means serving others with love and humility.

· · ·

Jesus' servanthood was also evident in His interactions with the marginalized and oppressed. He spent time with those society had cast aside—tax collectors, sinners, the sick, and the poor. He did not seek out the influential or the wealthy to build His kingdom but chose ordinary people, many of whom were overlooked or despised. By doing so, Jesus demonstrated that every person has inherent worth and value, regardless of their social status or past mistakes.

Embracing a servant's heart involves more than just occasional acts of kindness; it is a lifestyle characterized by continual self-giving and a posture of humility. This lifestyle can be cultivated through various practices and attitudes:

ACTIVE LISTENING: One of the first steps toward servanthood is learning to listen actively and empathetically to others. This means giving people our full attention, understanding their needs and concerns, and responding compassionately. By listening, we show respect and acknowledge the inherent value of each person.

ACTS OF SERVICE: Small, everyday service acts can significantly impact. This can include helping a neighbor with chores, volunteering at a local shelter, or offering encouragement. These acts of service reflect a heart willing to put others' needs before our own and demonstrate Christ's love in practical ways.

GENEROSITY: A servant's heart is marked by generosity. This is not limited to financial giving but includes sharing our time, talents, and resources. Being generous means going out of your way to help others, even when inconvenient or costly.

. . .

HUMILITY IN LEADERSHIP: For those in leadership positions, embracing servanthood means leading with humility and putting the well-being of others first. This involves recognizing that leadership is not about power or control but serving and empowering those we lead.

PRAYER AND DEPENDENCE ON GOD: Cultivating a servant's heart requires a deep connection. Through prayer, we seek His guidance and strength to serve others effectively. Dependence on God helps us maintain the proper perspective, reminding us that our ability to serve comes from His grace and provision.

FORGIVENESS AND GRACE: Embracing a servant's heart also involves forgiving and extending grace to others. This reflects the forgiveness and grace we have received from God and helps to build a community characterized by love and unity.

MENTORSHIP AND DISCIPLESHIP: Investing in the lives of others through mentorship and discipleship is a profound way to serve. By guiding and supporting others in their spiritual journeys, we help them grow in their faith and develop their servant hearts.

THE TRANSFORMATIVE POWER of servanthood lies in its ability to create a ripple effect of love and compassion. When we serve others, we meet their immediate needs and inspire them to serve. This creates a mutual care and support culture where each person is valued and uplifted.

. . .

MOREOVER, a community marked by servanthood reflects Christ's character in the world. In a society often driven by self-interest, such a community stands out as a beacon of hope and love. It demonstrates that true greatness is found not in what we achieve for ourselves but in what we give to others.

EMBRACING servanthood also profoundly impacts our spiritual growth. It helps us develop a more profound dependence on God as we recognize our need for His strength and guidance in serving others. It also fosters humility as we learn to put others' needs before our own and acknowledge that we are all equal before God.

SERVANTHOOD IS a vital aspect of Christlike living, rooted in humility and expressed through selfless acts of love and service. By following Jesus' example and embracing a servant's heart, we honor God and bring His love and grace to those around us. This radical approach to life transforms individuals and communities, creating a ripple effect of compassion and kindness reflecting God's heart.

Living Out Humility and Service

LIVING out humility and service is not merely theoretical but a practical reality to embrace daily. It requires intentionality, discipline, and a willingness to embrace discomfort and inconvenience for the sake of others. It means actively seeking out opportunities to serve through acts of kindness, expressions of love, or sacrificial giving.

. . .

PRACTICING humility and service begins with a mindset shift. It requires us to see others through the eyes of Christ, recognizing their inherent worth and dignity. This perspective helps us move beyond self-centeredness and develop a genuine concern for the well-being of others. Each day, we can intentionally look for ways to serve, from helping a colleague with a task to volunteering our time to a local charity.

ONE PRACTICAL WAY TO live out humility is through small acts of kindness. These acts may seem insignificant, but they can profoundly impact those who receive them. Whether it's offering a listening ear to someone going through a tough time, providing a word of encouragement, or simply being present for someone in need, these small gestures can brighten someone's day and demonstrate Christ's love in action. These acts of kindness reflect a heart willing to put others' needs before our own, a true mark of humility.

EXPRESSIONS OF LOVE are another powerful way to live out humility and service. As described in 1 Corinthians 13, love is patient, kind, and selfless. It seeks the good of others and rejoices in the truth. When we love others this way, we follow Christ's example, who loved us selflessly and sacrificially. This love can be shown in numerous ways, from spending quality time with loved ones to supporting a friend in their endeavors. By expressing love through our actions, we create an environment of care and support that reflects the heart of God.

SACRIFICIAL GIVING IS ALSO a key component of living out humility and service. This doesn't necessarily mean giving away all our possessions but being willing to share our resources with those in need. It could be financial support, but it also includes giving our time, talents, and energy. When we give sacrificially, we acknowledge that everything we have comes from God and are merely stewards of His blessings. This attitude of generosity reflects a humble recognition of our dependence on God and our desire to bless others as He has blessed us.

Living out humility and service also involves recognizing and valuing the contributions of others. It means fostering collaboration and cooperation, working together towards common goals. In a world that often values individual achievement, embracing a collaborative spirit can be challenging, but it is essential for creating a community that reflects Christ's love. By acknowledging the gifts and talents of others, we create an environment where everyone feels valued and appreciated. This recognition boosts the morale of those around us and encourages a culture of mutual respect and support.

Another crucial aspect of living out humility and service is creating spaces where everyone feels seen, heard, and valued. This means actively listening to others, acknowledging their experiences and perspectives, and creating an inclusive environment where everyone has a voice. It involves being attentive to the needs and concerns of others and responding with empathy and compassion. By doing so, we reflect the heart of Christ, who welcomed and valued every person, regardless of their status or position.

In our workplaces, living out humility and service might mean recognizing the contributions of team members, giving credit where it is due, and supporting colleagues in their professional growth. It involves creating a culture of respect and appreciation where everyone feels empowered to contribute their best. In our communities, it means engaging in acts of service that address the needs of those around us, from volunteering at local shelters to participating in community clean-up efforts. Though these actions may require effort and sacrifice, they demonstrate our commitment to serving others in tangible ways.

In our personal lives, living out humility and service involves being present for our families and friends, offering support and encouragement, and making time for meaningful connections. It means prioritizing relationships and being willing to put the needs of others before our own. This might look like offering to babysit for a busy parent, cooking a meal for a sick neighbor, or simply being available to listen and comfort a friend in distress.

Spiritual practices such as prayer and meditation can also help us cultivate humility and a servant's heart. By praying, we align our hearts with God's will and seek His guidance in serving others. Meditation on Scripture can remind us of Christ's example and inspire us to follow in His footsteps. These practices strengthen our relationship with God and equip us to serve others with a humble and willing heart.

Living out humility and service is a daily commitment that requires ongoing effort and intentionality. It involves being attentive to the needs of those around us and being willing to step out of our comfort zones to meet those needs. It means embracing opportunities to serve, no matter how small or inconvenient they may seem, and doing so with a heart full of love and compassion.

. . .

ULTIMATELY, living out humility and service is about embodying Christ's character daily. It's about reflecting His love, grace, and humility to those we encounter. When we choose to live this way, we not only impact the lives of others but also grow in our spiritual journey. We become more like Christ, who came not to be served but to serve and to give His life as a ransom for many.

LIVING out humility and service is a practical and powerful way to reflect Christ's love. It requires a deliberate effort to put others before ourselves, to recognize and value the contributions of those around us, and to create environments where everyone feels valued and respected. By embracing a servant's heart and living out humility in our daily interactions, we fulfill the call to be Christ's hands and feet in the world, bringing hope, love, and healing to those in need.

ULTIMATELY, humility and servanthood are virtues to be admired from a distance and qualities to be actively cultivated and embodied in our lives. By embracing these virtues, we reflect the character of our humble Savior and participate in His mission of reconciliation and redemption in the world. We witness the transformative power of God's love and grace through humility and service, bringing hope and healing to a broken and hurting world.

CHAPTER 7
DAILY WALK WITH CHRIST

∼

Developing a Consistent Spiritual Routine
Walking daily with Christ requires intentionality and consistency in cultivating spiritual practices that deepen our relationship with Him. Developing a consistent spiritual routine involves setting aside regular time for activities such as

prayer, meditation, and studying Scripture. This chapter will explore the importance of these practices and offer practical tips for integrating them into your daily life.

CREATING a spiritual routine begins with prioritizing your relationship with God. As we schedule time for work, exercise, and social activities, dedicating daily time to nurture our spiritual growth is essential. This can be achieved by setting aside specific times for spiritual practices, whether in the morning, during lunch breaks, or before bed. Consistency is vital; establishing a routine helps make these practices a natural and integral part of our lives.

ONE EFFECTIVE WAY TO develop a consistent spiritual routine is by creating a designated space for prayer and meditation. This space should be free from distractions and conducive to reflection and connection with God. It could be a quiet corner in your home, a cozy chair by a window, or even a spot in a nearby park. A dedicated space helps signal to your mind and body that it's time to focus on your spiritual life.

IN ADDITION to setting a regular time and place, using tools and resources that enhance your spiritual routine is helpful. Journals, holy books, and Bible study guides can provide structure and inspiration. Many people find that using a journal to record their prayers, reflections, and insights from Scripture enhances their spiritual practice. It allows for introspection and tracking spiritual growth over time.

. . .

A CONSISTENT SPIRITUAL routine involves prayer, meditation, Bible study, and regular corporate worship and fellowship participation. Engaging with a community of believers is vital for mutual encouragement and accountability. Attending church services, joining small groups, and participating in communal worship activities help reinforce our spiritual discipline and provide support from fellow Christians.

ENGAGING in spiritual practices such as fasting can also enhance our spiritual routine. Fasting involves abstaining from food or other distractions to focus on prayer and seek God's guidance. It's a way to humble ourselves before God, express our dependence on Him, and seek His intervention.

ANOTHER ASPECT of a consistent spiritual routine is practicing the Sabbath—a day set apart for rest and worship. Observing the Sabbath helps us pause from our busy schedules, reflect on God's goodness, and recharge spiritually. It's a reminder that our worth and identity are not based on our productivity but on our relationship with God.

INCORPORATING these practices into our daily and weekly routines requires discipline and intentionality. Setting realistic goals and gradually building up our spiritual habits is essential. Tracking our progress and celebrating small victories can help maintain motivation and commitment.

WE MUST REMAIN flexible and adaptable as we develop a consistent spiritual routine. Life's circumstances and responsibilities may change, requiring adjustments to our routines. The goal is to maintain a steadfast commitment to our relationship with God, even if the specific practices or schedules need to be modified.

INCORPORATING seasonal and annual rhythms into our spiritual routine can also be beneficial. Observing the liturgical calendar, celebrating Christian holidays, and participating in spiritual retreats provide deeper reflection and renewal opportunities. These rhythms help us connect with the broader Christian tradition and remind us of the significant events in Christ's and the church's lives.

DEVELOPING a consistent spiritual routine is ultimately about cultivating a heart that continually seeks God. It's about creating a lifestyle of worship, where every aspect of our lives is oriented toward Him. By prioritizing spiritual practices and integrating them into our daily lives, we grow in our relationship with Christ and become more attuned to His presence and guidance.

AS WE STRIVE to develop a consistent spiritual routine, we must seek God's help and rely on His grace. Spiritual disciplines are not about earning God's favor but positioning ourselves to receive His love and guidance. It's about cultivating a heart that desires to know Him more and to obey His will.

INCORPORATING gratitude into our spiritual routine can also transform our perspective and deepen our relationship with God. Practicing gratitude involves regularly acknowledging and giving thanks for God's big and small blessings. It shifts our focus from what we lack to what we have, fostering a sense of contentment and joy.

DEVELOPING a consistent spiritual routine involves growing closer to God and becoming more like Christ. It's about nurturing our spiritual lives in a way that impacts every aspect of who we are and how we live. By committing to regular prayer, meditation, and Scripture engagement, we build a strong foundation for our daily walk with Christ.

Importance of Prayer and Meditation

PRAYER AND MEDITATION are foundational practices in the daily walk with Christ. They foster a deep, personal connection with God and provide a means to express our thoughts, desires, and gratitude. We communicate with God through prayer, seeking His guidance, wisdom, and strength. Meditation allows us to quiet our minds and hearts, creating space to listen to God's voice and reflect on His Word.

THE IMPORTANCE of prayer cannot be overstated. Jesus Himself modeled a life of worship, often retreating to solitary places to commune with the Father (Luke 5:16). Prayer is not just about presenting our requests to God; it's also about aligning our hearts with His will. It's an opportunity to praise Him, confess our sins, and intercede for others. Developing a robust prayer life involves various forms of prayer, including adoration, confession, thanksgiving, and supplication (ACTS).

. . .

ADORATION FOCUSES on praising God for who He is—His attributes, character, and works. It shifts our focus from our circumstances to His greatness, fostering a sense of awe and reverence. Confession involves acknowledging our sins and shortcomings, seeking God's forgiveness, and repenting. This practice helps maintain a clear conscience and a right relationship with God.

THANKSGIVING IS EXPRESSING gratitude for God's blessings, both big and small. It cultivates a heart of thankfulness and helps us recognize God's faithfulness. Supplication involves presenting our needs and the needs of others to God. It's an act of dependence, acknowledging that we need God's intervention.

MEDITATION, however, involves dwelling on God's Word and His presence. It's about creating space to hear from God and reflect on His truths. Biblical meditation differs from other forms of meditation in that it focuses on Scripture and seeks to internalize God's Word. Psalm 1:2 speaks of the blessedness of those whose delight is in the law of the Lord and who meditate on His law day and night.

THE DISCIPLINE of prayer and meditation extends beyond personal devotion and involves intercessory prayer for others. Intercessory prayer involves praying for others and lifting their needs and concerns before God. It's a powerful way to support and encourage others, especially those facing difficult circumstances. We participate in God's healing, restoration, and transformation work by praying for others.

. . .

PRACTICING solitude and silence is another aspect of meditation that can deepen our connection with God. In our noisy and fast-paced world, finding moments of silence allows us to tune out distractions and focus on God's presence. Solitude allows us to reflect, listen to God's voice, and gain clarity and direction.

ENGAGING IN CONTEMPLATIVE PRAYER, such as centering prayer or the practice of the Examen, can also enhance our prayer life. Centering prayer involves focusing on a sacred word or phrase that helps center our thoughts on God. The Examen, a practice developed by St. Ignatius of Loyola, consists of reflecting on the day's events and discerning God's presence and guidance.

INCORPORATING these diverse forms of prayer and meditation into our spiritual routine enriches our relationship with God and helps us grow in spiritual maturity. It allows us to experience the fullness of God's presence and align our lives with His will.

PRAYER AND MEDITATION also play a crucial role in spiritual discernment. As we seek God's guidance for decisions and direction, prayer and meditation help us attune our hearts to His will. Through prayerful reflection and listening, we gain clarity and insight, allowing us to make decisions that align with God's purposes.

PRAYER AND MEDITATION provide comfort and strength in times of difficulty and uncertainty. They remind us of God's sovereignty and faithfulness, helping us trust His plans even when circumstances are challenging. Praying and meditating helps us find peace and assurance in God's presence.

ENGAGING in communal prayer and meditation can also strengthen our spiritual walk. Joining prayer groups, participating in prayer chains, and attending prayer meetings allow us to connect with other believers and share our burdens and joys. Corporate prayer fosters a sense of unity and mutual support, reminding us that we are part of a larger body of Christ.

PRACTICING prayer and meditation also cultivates a spirit of dependence on God. It reminds us that we are not self-sufficient but reliant on His grace and provision. We acknowledge our need for God's guidance, strength, and wisdom in prayer. Meditation helps us internalize His truths and rely on His promises.

PRAYER AND MEDITATION also nurture a heart of worship. As we spend time in God's presence, we are drawn to worship Him for who He is and what He has done. This worship extends beyond formal settings to become a way of life where our thoughts, words, and actions reflect our love and reverence for God.

MAINTAINING a consistent practice of prayer and meditation can be especially important in times of spiritual dryness or struggle. These practices anchor us in God's faithfulness and help us persevere through difficult seasons. They remind us of His unchanging nature and constant presence, providing hope and encouragement.

Integrating Scripture into Daily Life

INTEGRATING Scripture into daily life is essential for spiritual growth and alignment with God's will. The Bible is God's revealed Word, providing guidance, wisdom, and insight for every aspect of life. By immersing ourselves in Scripture, we gain a deeper understanding of God's character, His promises, and His commands.

A PRACTICAL WAY TO integrate Scripture into daily life is through regular Bible reading and study. This involves more than just reading a few verses daily; it requires thoughtful engagement with the text. Setting aside time each day to read the Bible systematically helps ensure we are exposed to the whole counsel of God's Word. Many people find reading plans that guide them through the entire Bible in a year or focus on specific themes or books helpful.

IN ADDITION TO REGULAR READING, studying Scripture in depth is crucial. This involves examining the context, understanding the original meaning, and applying the lessons to our lives. Resources like study Bibles, commentaries, and Bible dictionaries can aid this process. Joining a Bible study group allows one to learn from others, share insights, and hold each other accountable.

MEMORIZING Scripture is another effective way to integrate God's Word into daily life. Psalm 119:11 says, "I have hidden your word in my heart that I might not sin against you." Memorization helps us internalize God's truths, making them readily available in times of need. It allows us to meditate on Scripture throughout the day, bringing God's promises and commands to mind in various situations.

. . .

THE ULTIMATE GOAL of Bible reading and study is applying Scripture to our daily lives. James 1:22 encourages us to be doers of the Word, not hearers only. This involves allowing God's Word to shape our thoughts, attitudes, and actions. It means seeking to live out the principles and commands of Scripture in our relationships, work, and decision-making.

IN ADDITION to regular Bible reading and study, integrating Scripture into daily life involves using it as a guide for prayer. Praying Scripture means using the words of the Bible to shape our prayers. This practice helps us align our desires and requests with God's will and ensures our prayers are rooted in His Word.

FOR EXAMPLE, praying the Psalms allows us to express various emotions and experiences, from praise and thanksgiving to lament and petition. The prayers of Paul in the New Testament provide rich theological insights and can be adapted for personal and intercessory prayer. By praying Scripture, we deepen our engagement with God's Word and enrich our prayer life.

INCORPORATING Scripture into our conversations and interactions with others is another way to integrate it into daily life. Sharing Bible verses, discussing biblical principles, and encouraging others with God's promises can profoundly impact. It helps create a faith culture and promotes spiritual growth within our communities.

. . .

USING technology can also help integrate Scripture into our daily routines. Bible apps, online devotionals, and podcasts provide convenient access to God's Word and spiritual resources. Setting reminders or alarms for prayer and Bible reading times can help maintain consistency and accountability.

TO INTEGRATE Scripture into our daily lives effectively, it's helpful to approach it with a teachable and humble heart. Being open to the Holy Spirit's guidance and allowing Scripture to challenge and transform us is essential. It means approaching the Bible as a text to be read and as God's living Word that speaks into our lives.

ENGAGING with Scripture creatively can also enhance our understanding and application. Practices such as lectio divina, a method of meditative reading, help us slow down and savor the Word. Creative expressions like journaling, drawing, or writing poetry inspired by Scripture can deepen our connection with God's Word and allow us to explore its meaning personally and profoundly.

SHARING our insights and experiences with Scripture in community settings can also be enriching. Participating in Bible study groups, small group discussions, and teaching opportunities allows us to learn from others and grow together. It fosters a sense of accountability and encourages us to apply God's Word practically.

TO TRULY INTEGRATE Scripture into daily life, it's essential to approach it with a heart willing to obey. James 1:22-25 emphasizes the importance of being doers of the Word and not hearers only. This means allowing God's Word to shape our actions, decisions, and interactions with others.

Engaging with Scripture in community settings can also provide opportunities for accountability and mutual encouragement. Discussing biblical principles and their application in small groups or Bible studies helps us learn from others and gain new perspectives. It fosters a sense of community and shared growth.

Incorporating Scripture into family life is another powerful way to integrate it into daily routines. Reading the Bible together, discussing its meaning, and praying as a family create a foundation of faith and spiritual growth. It helps instill biblical values and principles in children and encourages open conversations about faith.

Integrating Scripture into daily life involves a wholehearted commitment to living according to God's Word. It means allowing His truths to guide our decisions, shape our character, and influence our interactions with others. Doing so reflects Christ's love and wisdom in every aspect of our lives.

Developing a consistent spiritual routine, prioritizing prayer and meditation, and integrating Scripture into daily life is essential for a fruitful walk with Christ. These practices deepen our relationship with God, align our hearts with His will, and empower us to live out our faith practically. Committing to these spiritual disciplines nurtures a vibrant and growing relationship with Christ, transforming our lives and impacting those around us.

"HOW TO BE CHRISTLIKE"

CHAPTER 8

CHRISTLIKE RELATIONSHIPS

B uilding and maintaining relationships based on Christ's example is a cornerstone of Christlike life. These relationships, founded on love, grace, and forgiveness, reflect the heart of Jesus' teachings. This chapter will explore how to build

Christlike relationships, handle conflict with grace and forgiveness, and encourage and uplift others in our daily interactions.

Building Relationships Based on Christ's Example

BUILDING relationships that mirror Christ's example involves cultivating a deep love and respect for others. Jesus' life and ministry were characterized by His profound ability to connect with people from all walks of life, showing them unconditional love and acceptance. To build such relationships, we must first understand the principles that guided Jesus' interactions.

Unconditional Love and Acceptance

JESUS DEMONSTRATED unconditional love and acceptance towards everyone He encountered, regardless of their social status, background, or past mistakes. He reached out to tax collectors, prostitutes, and sinners, offering them a chance to experience God's love and grace. This unconditional love is the foundation of Christlike relationships. It requires us to look beyond people's flaws and imperfections and to love them as they are.

PRACTICALLY, this means extending kindness and patience to others, even when it is difficult. It involves being slow to judge and quick to forgive, recognizing that everyone is a work in progress. By loving others unconditionally, we create an environment where people feel valued and accepted, fostering more profound and meaningful connections.

Empathy and Compassion

ANOTHER CRITICAL ELEMENT in building Christlike relationships is empathy. Jesus was deeply empathetic, always putting Himself in the shoes of others and feeling their pain and joy. We can better understand and connect with those around us by developing empathy. This involves actively listening to others, validating their feelings, and showing genuine concern for their well-being.

EMPATHY REQUIRES us to be present and attentive, to listen without interrupting or offering unsolicited advice. It means being there for others in need, offering support and understanding. By practicing empathy, we build trust and strengthen our relationships, creating a sense of solidarity and mutual respect.

Servant Leadership

JESUS TAUGHT that authentic leadership is found in serving others. He demonstrated this through acts of service, such as washing His disciples' feet. We should strive to serve others selflessly in our relationships, putting their needs above ours. This servant leadership fosters mutual respect and strengthens the bonds between individuals.

SERVANT LEADERSHIP INVOLVES TAKING the initiative to meet the needs of others, whether through acts of kindness, providing assistance, or offering encouragement. It means leading by example and showing others what it means to live a life of humility and service. By adopting a servant's heart, we inspire others to do the same, creating a ripple effect of kindness and generosity.

. . .

Trust and Integrity

TRUST IS a fundamental component of any healthy relationship. Jesus was trustworthy and always acted with integrity. To build Christlike relationships, we must be honest, reliable, and consistent in our actions. This creates a safe and stable environment where relationships can thrive.

INTEGRITY MEANS BEING true to our word, keeping our promises, and acting honestly and transparently. It involves being dependable and accountable, owning up to our mistakes, and making amends when necessary. Demonstrating integrity builds trust and credibility, essential for solid and lasting relationships.

Forgiveness and Reconciliation

FORGIVENESS IS at the heart of Christ's teachings. Jesus taught that we must forgive others as God has forgiven us. In our relationships, we should be quick to forgive and seek reconciliation when conflicts arise. This not only heals wounds but also strengthens our bonds with others.

FORGIVENESS INVOLVES LETTING GO of resentment and bitterness, releasing the hurt, and extending grace to those who have wronged us. It means restoring broken relationships through open, honest communication, understanding, and compassion. By practicing forgiveness, we experience freedom and peace and pave the way for healing and reconciliation.

. . .

Patience and Understanding

Jesus showed incredible patience and understanding in His interactions with others. He was patient with His disciples as they struggled to grasp His teachings and extended grace to those who made mistakes. In our relationships, practicing patience means giving others the time and space to grow and learn. It involves understanding that everyone is on their journey and that growth takes time.

Patience requires us to be slow to anger and quick to listen, to refrain from rushing to judgment or jumping to conclusions. It means accepting others for who they are, recognizing their strengths and weaknesses, and supporting their growth and development. By practicing patience, we create an atmosphere of acceptance and encouragement where relationships can flourish.

Humility and Selflessness

Humility is a hallmark of Christlike relationships. Despite being God's Son, Jesus humbled Himself and served others. He put the needs of others before His own, demonstrating true selflessness. In our relationships, we should strive to be humble, recognizing that we are not above others and are called to serve.

Humility involves acknowledging our limitations and weaknesses, being willing to learn from others, and valuing their contributions. It means putting the needs of others before our desires and ambitions and seeking to uplift and support them. By practicing humility, we build relationships based on mutual respect and admiration.

Communication and Openness

EFFECTIVE COMMUNICATION IS vital in building strong relationships. Jesus was open and honest in His communication, often using parables and stories to convey profound truths. In our relationships, we should strive to communicate openly and honestly, sharing our thoughts and feelings while being receptive to others.

COMMUNICATION INVOLVES ACTIVE LISTENING, expressing ourselves clearly and respectfully, and being open to feedback. It means being willing to engage in difficult conversations and addressing issues and concerns with honesty and empathy. Fostering open and honest communication builds trust and understanding, creating a solid foundation for our relationships.

Handling Conflict with Grace and Forgiveness

CONFLICTS ARE inevitable in any relationship. However, handling these conflicts with grace and forgiveness sets Christlike relationships apart. Jesus provided clear guidance on approaching disputes, emphasizing the importance of grace, patience, and forgiveness.

Approaching Conflict with Humility

WHEN CONFLICTS ARISE, we must approach them humbly, acknowledging our faults and being open to correction. Jesus taught us to examine ourselves before addressing someone else's shortcomings (Matthew 7:3-5). This humble approach helps to de-escalate tensions and fosters a more constructive dialogue.

APPROACHING conflict with humility involves recognizing our contributions to the problem, being willing to admit our mistakes, and seeking to understand the other person's perspective. It means being open to feedback and correction and willing to make changes and compromises for the sake of the relationship.

Active Listening and Understanding

EFFECTIVE CONFLICT RESOLUTION begins with active listening. We can understand their concerns and feelings by genuinely listening to the other person's perspective. This understanding paves the way for finding common ground and resolving differences.

ACTIVE LISTENING INVOLVES GIVING the other person our full attention, refraining from interrupting or judging and seeking to understand their point of view. It means validating their feelings and concerns, showing empathy, and being willing to consider their perspective. By practicing active listening, we build trust and create an environment where conflicts can be resolved constructively.

Speaking the Truth in Love

JESUS EMPHASIZED the importance of speaking the truth in love (Ephesians 4:15), Which means addressing conflicts honestly but with kindness and respect. Harsh words and accusations only escalate conflicts, whereas gentle and loving communication can lead to resolution and healing.

SPEAKING the truth in love involves being honest, direct, considerate, and compassionate. It means sensitively addressing issues and concerns, avoiding blame and criticism, and finding solutions. By speaking the truth in love, we create a safe and respectful environment where conflicts can be resolved effectively.

Seeking Forgiveness and Offering It Freely

A KEY ASPECT of handling conflict Christlike is seeking forgiveness when we have wronged others and being willing to forgive those who wronged us. Jesus' parable of the unforgiving servant (Matthew 18:21-35) underscores the importance of forgiving others as God has forgiven us.

SEEKING forgiveness involves acknowledging our mistakes, taking responsibility for our actions, and expressing genuine remorse. It means making amends and seeking to restore the relationship. Offering forgiveness consists of letting go of resentment and bitterness, releasing the hurt, and extending grace to those who have wronged us. By practicing forgiveness, we experience freedom and peace and pave the way for healing and reconciliation.

Prayer and Reflection

PRAYER IS a powerful tool in handling conflicts. By bringing our concerns and grievances to God, we can gain clarity and wisdom on how to proceed. Prayer also helps to soften our hearts and open us to the possibility of reconciliation.

PRAYER AND REFLECTION involve seeking God's guidance and wisdom, asking for His help resolving conflicts, and being open to His leading. It means taking time to reflect on the situation, considering the other person's perspective, and seeking to understand God's will. By praying and reflecting, we invite God's presence into the conflict and allow Him to work in our hearts and minds.

Mediation and Peacemaking

IN SOME CASES, conflicts may require mediation from a neutral third party. Jesus taught that blessed are the peacemakers (Matthew 5:9). Seeking the help of a mediator or counselor can provide a fresh perspective and facilitate resolution. Peacemakers help to bridge gaps, foster understanding, and bring about reconciliation.

MEDIATION INVOLVES SEEKING the assistance of a neutral third party to help resolve the conflict. This can be a trusted friend, a counselor, or a pastor. The mediator helps to facilitate communication, provide perspective, and guide the parties toward a resolution. Peacemaking involves taking proactive steps to resolve conflicts, seeking to restore relationships, and promoting harmony.

Maintaining a Spirit of Grace

GRACE IS the unmerited favor that God extends to us, and it should be a hallmark of our relationships. Extending grace means showing kindness and mercy, even when it's undeserved. It involves letting go of grudges and acting with love and compassion.

MAINTAINING a spirit of grace involves being patient and understanding, showing kindness and compassion, and forgiving. It means responding to conflicts with love and grace, even when difficult. By maintaining a spirit of grace, we reflect the heart of Christ and create an environment where disputes can be resolved constructively.

Setting Healthy Boundaries

WHILE FORGIVENESS and grace are crucial, setting healthy boundaries in relationships is also essential. Jesus set boundaries, often withdrawing to solitary places to pray and recharge. Boundaries protect our well-being and ensure that relationships remain respectful and mutually beneficial.

SETTING healthy boundaries involves being transparent about our needs and limits, communicating them to others, and being willing to enforce them. It means taking responsibility for our well-being and ensuring our relationships are respectful and supportive. By setting healthy boundaries, we create an environment where relationships can thrive.

Long-term Reconciliation

TRUE RECONCILIATION GOES beyond a simple apology. It involves a long-term commitment to rebuilding trust and repairing relationships. This process takes time and effort but leads to stronger, healthier relationships in the long run.

LONG-TERM RECONCILIATION INVOLVES COMMITTING to the relationship, working through issues and challenges, and restoring trust and intimacy. It means being patient and persistent, showing grace and understanding, and being willing to forgive and seek forgiveness. By committing to long-term reconciliation, we build strong and resilient relationships.

Encouraging and Uplifting Others

ENCOURAGEMENT AND SUPPORT are vital components of Christlike relationships. Jesus often encouraged His disciples, strengthening their faith and helping them to overcome challenges. By encouraging and uplifting others, we can profoundly impact their lives and strengthen our relationships.

Offering Words of Affirmation

WORDS HAVE the power to build up or tear down. Jesus often used words to affirm and encourage those around Him. In our relationships, we should offer words of affirmation, recognizing and appreciating the strengths and efforts of others.

OFFERING words of affirmation involves being intentional about expressing appreciation and encouragement. It means recognizing and acknowledging the efforts and accomplishments of others and expressing our appreciation sincerely and meaningfully. By offering words of affirmation, we build confidence and strengthen our relationships.

Being Present and Available

ONE OF THE most significant ways to encourage and uplift others is by being present and available. Jesus was always there for His disciples, providing guidance, comfort, and support. We show them they are valued and loved by making ourselves available to listen and help others.

BEING present and available involves being attentive and responsive to others' needs. It means making time for our relationships, being willing to listen and offer support, and being there for others in need. By being present and available, we build trust and strengthen our relationships.

Acts of Kindness and Service

ACTS OF KINDNESS and service are tangible expressions of our love and support. Jesus' life was marked by acts of kindness, from healing the sick to feeding the hungry. Small acts of kindness can significantly impact our relationships, showing others we care about their well-being.

ACTS OF KINDNESS and service involve taking the initiative to meet the needs of others, whether through practical assistance, thoughtful gestures, or acts of generosity. They mean being willing to go out of our way to help others and show them that they are valued and appreciated. We build strong and supportive relationships by practicing acts of kindness and service.

Praying for Others

PRAYER IS a powerful way to support and uplift others. We can invite God's presence and blessings into their lives by praying for our friends, family, and even those with whom we have conflicts. Prayer also helps to strengthen our faith and trust in God's ability to work in the lives of others.

PRAYING for others involves lifting their needs and concerns to God, asking for His guidance and intervention, and seeking His blessings and protection. It means being faithful in our prayers and willing to intercede on behalf of others. By praying for others, we build a strong spiritual connection and support each other in our faith journey.

Providing Support and Encouragement in Difficult Times

LIFE IS full of challenges and difficult times. Jesus often provided support and encouragement to those who were struggling. Being there for others during tough times, offering a listening ear, a shoulder to cry on, or practical help can make a significant difference in our relationships.

PROVIDING support and encouragement in difficult times involves being willing to step in and offer help and support when needed. It means being compassionate, understanding, and willing to offer practical assistance and emotional support. By providing support and encouragement, we build strong and resilient relationships.

Celebrating Successes and Milestones

CELEBRATING the successes and milestones of others is a powerful way to encourage and uplift them. Whether it's a personal achievement, a career milestone, or a spiritual victory, acknowledging and celebrating these moments fosters a sense of community and mutual support.

CELEBRATING successes and milestones involves being attentive to and willing to acknowledge and celebrate others' achievements and milestones. It means expressing our joy and appreciation and being willing to share in their successes. By celebrating achievements and milestones, we build a solid and supportive community.

Offering Constructive Feedback

WHILE AFFIRMATION and encouragement are essential, so is offering constructive feedback. Jesus often provided guidance and correction to His disciples, helping them grow and improve. In our relationships, giving feedback with kindness and love can help others develop and reach their full potential.

OFFERING constructive feedback involves being honest, direct, considerate, and compassionate. It means providing feedback in a helpful, supportive way and being willing to offer guidance and support. Giving constructive feedback, we help others grow, develop, and build strong and supportive relationships.

Building a Supportive Community

CREATING an environment of support and encouragement requires building a community that values and practices these principles. This involves fostering relationships based on mutual respect, love, and a shared commitment to growth and well-being.

BUILDING a supportive community involves intentionally creating an environment where everyone feels valued and supported. It means being willing to invest in our relationships, being open and honest in communication, and offering help and support. Building a supportive community creates an environment where everyone can thrive.

Modeling Christlike Behavior

ULTIMATELY, modeling Christlike behavior is the most potent way to encourage and uplift others. By living out the principles of love, grace, humility, and service, we inspire others to do the same. Our actions speak louder than words and can have a lasting impact on those around us.

MODELING CHRISTLIKE BEHAVIOR involves intentionally living out our faith in our daily lives. It means being willing to put others first, to serve with humility and grace, and to show love and compassion.

By modeling Christlike behavior, we inspire others to do the same and create an environment where everyone can thrive.

Building Christlike relationships involves embodying the love, humility, and grace Jesus demonstrated throughout His life. By understanding Christ's example, handling conflicts with grace and forgiveness, and encouraging and uplifting others, we can develop deep, meaningful relationships that reflect the heart of Jesus. These relationships enrich our lives and serve as a powerful testimony to the love and grace of God in a world that desperately needs it. We can build relationships that honor God and transform our communities through intentional effort, prayer, and a commitment to Christlike principles.

CHAPTER 9
SERVICE AND MISSION

The Call to Serve

S ervice is a fundamental aspect of Christlike living, deeply rooted in the teachings and example of Jesus Christ. Throughout His ministry, Jesus consistently demonstrated the importance of serving others, emphasizing that true greatness is found in humility and selflessness. He overturned societal norms by washing His disciples' feet, which were traditionally reserved for the lowest servants. This powerful act of humility and service, recorded in John 13:1-17, illustrates that no act of service is beneath us and that authentic leadership is marked by a willingness to serve others.

JESUS' life was a continual demonstration of service. From healing the sick and feeding the hungry to comforting the grieving and teaching the masses, His actions were driven by a profound love and compassion for humanity. In Mark 10:45, Jesus stated, "For even the Son of Man did not come to be served, but to serve, and to give His life as a ransom for many." This declaration highlights that the essence of His mission was service, culminating in the ultimate act of love—His sacrificial death on the cross.

THE CALL TO serve is not limited to a select few; it is a universal mandate for all believers. Jesus' teachings make it clear that followers are called to serve others. In the parable of the Good Samaritan (Luke 10:25-37), Jesus redefines what it means to be a neighbor, emphasizing that we are to show mercy and compassion to anyone in need, regardless of their background or status. This parable underscores that service transcends social and cultural boundaries, calling us to act with kindness and love toward all people.

. . .

UNDERSTANDING this call involves recognizing that service expresses our love for God and our neighbors. As stated by Jesus in Matthew 22:37-39, the greatest commandments are to love God with all our heart, soul, and mind and to love our neighbor as ourselves. Service is a tangible manifestation of these commandments. When we serve others, we live out our love for God by reflecting His love to those around us. Service becomes an act of worship, a way to honor God by caring for His creation and embodying His love in our actions.

MOREOVER, service is integral to the health and growth of the Christian community. The Apostle Paul, in his letters to the early churches, frequently exhorted believers to serve one another. In Galatians 5:13, he writes, "You, my brothers and sisters, were called to be free. But do not use your freedom to indulge the flesh; rather, serve one another humbly in love." Paul's teachings emphasize that service is not just an individual responsibility but a communal one. It is through serving each other that the body of Christ is built up and strengthened.

SERVICE ALSO PLAYS a crucial role in personal spiritual growth. By serving others, we develop qualities such as humility, compassion, and patience. These virtues are essential for our spiritual formation and bring us closer to the character of Christ. Serving allows us to step outside of our concerns and connect with the needs and struggles of others, fostering a sense of empathy and community. It challenges us to live out our faith in practical ways, reinforcing the lessons of scripture through action.

. . .

However, service has its challenges. It can be demanding, requiring time, energy, and sometimes sacrifice. Yet, the rewards of service are profound. Not only do we make a positive impact on others' lives, but we also experience personal fulfillment and growth. Service can transform us, deepening our faith and broadening our understanding of God's love and grace.

Service is a fundamental aspect of Christlike living. It is deeply rooted in the teachings and example of Jesus Christ, who emphasized that true greatness is found in humility and selflessness. The call to serve is universal, extending to all believers as a tangible expression of our love for God and our neighbors. Through service, we worship God, build the Christian community, and experience personal spiritual growth. Despite its challenges, service rewards are immense, offering fulfillment and transformation for both the giver and the receiver.

Biblical Foundation of Service

The Bible is replete with teachings on the importance of service, highlighting it as a core tenet of the Christian faith. Throughout both the Old and New Testaments, scripture consistently emphasizes that serving others is a vital expression of love, humility, and obedience to God.

Jesus Himself set the ultimate example by washing His disciples' feet, an act of profound humility and love recorded in John 13:1-17. This event occurred during the Last Supper, a significant moment when Jesus was fully aware of the suffering He was about to endure. Despite His imminent crucifixion, Jesus chose to perform this humble task, typically reserved for the lowest of servants. By washing His disciples' feet, Jesus demonstrated that true greatness in the Kingdom of God is measured not by power or status but by one's willingness to serve others selflessly. His actions were a powerful reminder that leaders in His Kingdom are called to serve, not to be served.

IN MATTHEW 20:26-28, Jesus explicitly taught that the greatest among us would be the one who serves. When the mother of James and John asked Jesus to grant her sons positions of honor in His Kingdom, Jesus used the opportunity to teach a profound lesson on leadership and service. He said, "Whoever wants to become great among you must be your servant, and whoever wants to be first must be your slave—just as the Son of Man did not come to be served, but to serve, and to give his life as a ransom for many." This principle turns worldly concepts of greatness and authority on their head, establishing that in the Kingdom of God, true greatness is found in humility and service to others.

THIS PRINCIPLE of service is echoed throughout the New Testament, where believers are encouraged to serve one another in love. Galatians 5:13 emphasizes that Christians are called to freedom, but this freedom is not an excuse for self-indulgence; instead, it is an opportunity to serve others humbly in love. Paul writes, "You, my brothers and sisters, were called to be free. But do not use your freedom to indulge the flesh; rather, serve one another humbly in love." This call to service is an integral part of living out our faith and demonstrating the love of Christ to others.

. . .

FURTHERMORE, 1 Peter 4:10 underscores the importance of using our gifts for the common good. The apostle Peter encourages believers to use whatever gifts they have received to serve others, faithfully administering God's grace in its various forms. He writes, "Each of you should use whatever gift you have received to serve others as faithful stewards of God's grace in its various forms." This passage highlights that every believer has been endowed with unique gifts and talents, which should be used not for personal gain but for the benefit of others and the glory of God.

THE NEW TESTAMENT also provides numerous examples of early Christians living out this call to service. In Acts 6:1-7, the apostles appointed seven men to oversee the daily food distribution to widows, ensuring the community's physical needs were met. This service allowed the apostles to focus on prayer and the ministry of the word, demonstrating the importance of both spiritual and practical service in the church's life. Similarly, in Romans 12:6-8, Paul lists various gifts, including serving, teaching, encouraging, giving, leading, and showing mercy, urging believers to use these gifts diligently and cheerfully to build up the body of Christ.

THE EMPHASIS on service extends beyond specific acts of kindness to encompass a broader attitude of humility and selflessness. Philippians 2:3-4 exhorts believers to "do nothing out of selfish ambition or vain conceit. Rather, in humility, value others above yourselves, not looking to your interests but each of you to the interests of the others." This mindset of putting others first is central to the Christian service ethic, reflecting the heart of Jesus' teachings and example.

. . .

THE BIBLE IS FILLED with teachings on the importance of service, with Jesus Himself setting the ultimate example through His life and actions. By washing His disciples' feet and teaching that the greatest among us are those who serve, Jesus established a model of humble service that believers are called to follow. This principle is reinforced throughout the New Testament, where believers are encouraged to serve one another in love and to use their gifts for the common good. Embracing this call to service is essential for living out our faith and embodying the love and humility of Christ in our daily lives.

Service as Worship

Service is not just an act of charity but a profound form of worship that deeply intertwines with our spiritual lives. When we serve others, we honor God and reflect His love and compassion in tangible ways. This concept is beautifully encapsulated in Romans 12:1, where Paul urges believers to "offer your bodies as a living sacrifice, holy and pleasing to God—this is your true and proper worship." This passage emphasizes that our everyday actions, including acts of service, are integral to our spiritual lives and worship.

THE IDEA of service as worship underscores the holistic nature of Christian devotion. Worship is not confined to Sunday services or specific religious rituals; it permeates every aspect of our lives. We express our gratitude to God and our commitment to His teachings by serving others. Each act of kindness, generosity, and support becomes a spiritual offering, demonstrating our faith in action.

Service as a Living Sacrifice

IN THE OLD TESTAMENT, sacrifices were a primary way of worshiping God, offering animals or other goods at the temple. These sacrifices were symbols of atonement and devotion. Paul transforms this concept in the New Testament, calling believers to present themselves as living sacrifices. This means dedicating our lives to God in every action and decision, including how we interact with and serve others. This living sacrifice is not a one-time event but a continual process of surrender and service, reflecting our ongoing relationship with God.

Reflecting God's Love and Compassion

SERVICE ALLOWS us to embody God's attributes in our interactions with others. Jesus' ministry was marked by acts of compassion, healing the sick, feeding the hungry, and comforting the brokenhearted. We mirror these actions when we engage in service, becoming vessels of God's love and compassion. This reflection of divine love is a powerful testimony of our faith, demonstrating Christ's character to the world.

Integrating Service into Everyday Life

VIEWING service as worship encourages us to integrate acts of kindness and assistance into our daily routines. It shifts our perspective from seeing service as an occasional duty to recognizing it as a fundamental aspect of our spiritual practice. Whether it is helping a neighbor, volunteering at a local charity, or simply offering a listening ear to someone in need, these acts become expressions of our devotion to God. This integration transforms our daily lives into a continuous act of worship, where every moment presents an opportunity to honor God through service.

. . .

The Impact of Service on Spiritual Growth

ENGAGING in service has a transformative effect on our spiritual growth. It fosters humility, as we put others' needs before our own. It cultivates empathy as we connect with the struggles and joys of those we serve. It strengthens our faith as we see God's hand at work through our actions and witness His love's impact on others' lives. By prioritizing service, we open ourselves to deeper spiritual insights and experiences, drawing closer to God as we follow His example of love and compassion.

Service as a Community Practice

SERVICE ALSO PLAYS a crucial role in building and strengthening the Christian community. When believers come together to serve, it fosters unity and cooperation. Shared service projects and initiatives create bonds of fellowship and mutual support, enhancing the sense of community within the church. This communal aspect of service amplifies its impact, as collective efforts can address more extensive needs and make a more significant difference. Moreover, it provides a witness to the broader community, showcasing the church's commitment to living out the teachings of Christ.

SERVICE IS a vital and profound form of worship that extends beyond acts of charity to encompass our spiritual lives. By serving others, we honor God, reflect His love and compassion, and integrate our faith into everyday actions. Romans 12:1 calls us to be living sacrifices, highlighting that our everyday actions, including acts of service, are integral to our worship. Embracing this perspective transforms our approach to service, enriching our spiritual growth, fostering community, and drawing us closer to God as we live out His call to love and serve others.

Motivation for Service

OUR MOTIVATION for service should be rooted in gratitude for God's grace and love. We serve not to earn salvation or favor but as a response to the incredible love we have received. Genuine service flows from a heart transformed by Christ, desiring to share His love and grace with others.

Challenges and Rewards of Service

WHILE THE CALL TO serve is clear, it has challenges. Serving others can be demanding, requiring time, energy, and sometimes sacrifice. However, the rewards of service are profound. Not only do we positively impact others' lives, but we also grow spiritually, experiencing the joy and fulfillment that comes from following Jesus' example.

FINDING YOUR MISSION Field

Discovering where and how to serve effectively involves discerning your unique calling and mission. This process includes self-reflection, prayer, and an openness to God's leading. Each person's mission field may look different, depending on their gifts, passions, and circumstances.

Identifying Your Gifts and Passions

GOD HAS UNIQUELY GIFTED us with talents and passions that can be used for His glory. Identifying these gifts is the first step in finding your mission field. Reflect on your skills, experiences, and what brings you joy and fulfillment. Consider how these can be applied in service to others. Spiritual gifts inventories and personality assessments can also provide insights into your strengths.

Listening to God's Call

DISCERNING your mission field requires attentive listening to God's voice. Spend prayer, asking God to reveal where He calls you to serve. Pay attention to the needs around you and any burdens or passions that God places on your heart. Sometimes, God's call may come through opportunities presented by others or a deep conviction to address a specific issue or need.

Understanding the Needs Around You

YOUR MISSION FIELD is often found where your gifts and passions intersect with the needs of others. Look around your community, workplace, and social circles to identify areas where you can make a difference. Understanding these specific needs helps direct your efforts and ensures that your service is impactful and relevant.

Being Open to Change

YOUR MISSION FIELD may change as you grow and circumstances evolve. Be open to God's leading and willing to step into new service areas as He directs. Flexibility and a willingness to adapt are essential for effective service.

. . .

Engaging with Your Community

BUILDING relationships within your community is crucial for effective service. Engage with local organizations, churches, and community groups to understand their needs and how you can contribute. Collaboration and partnership with others enhance the impact of your efforts and create a supportive network for sustained service.

PRACTICAL WAYS TO Serve in Your Community

There are countless ways to serve in your community, each offering opportunities to make a meaningful impact. The following are practical suggestions for engaging in service, categorized by different areas of need.

Supporting the Vulnerable

- **Homeless Shelters and Food Banks**: Volunteer your time at local shelters and food banks, helping to distribute food, prepare meals, or provide support services.
- **Clothing Drives**: Organize or participate in clothing drives to collect and distribute clothing to needy people.
- **Mentorship Programs**: Become a mentor to at-risk youth or adults, offering guidance, support, and positive role modeling.

Education and Youth Services

- **Tutoring and After-School Programs**: Volunteer as a tutor or helper in after-school programs, assisting students with their studies and providing a safe and supportive environment.
- **School Partnerships**: Partner with local schools to support their needs, such as providing supplies, organizing events, or offering extracurricular activities.
- **Youth Groups and Camps**: Get involved in church or community youth groups and camps, helping to lead activities, teach lessons, and build relationships with young people.

Health and Wellness

- **Medical Missions**: If you have medical training, participate in local or international medical missions, providing healthcare services to underserved populations.
- **Health Education**: Offer workshops or seminars on health topics, such as nutrition, exercise, mental health, and disease prevention.
- **Support Groups**: Facilitate or join support groups for individuals dealing with health issues, addiction, or other challenges. These groups provide a safe space for sharing and encouragement.

Environmental Stewardship

- **Community Cleanups**: Organize or join community cleanup efforts to remove litter, beautify public spaces, and promote environmental awareness.
- **Recycling Programs**: Support or start recycling initiatives in your community, educating others on the importance of recycling and how to do it effectively.
- **Sustainable Practices**: Advocate for and implement sustainable practices in your community, such as community gardens, composting, and conservation projects.

Faith-Based Initiatives

- **Church Ministries**: Serve in various church ministries, such as hospitality, worship, children's programs, and outreach efforts.
- **Mission Trips:** Participate in short-term or long-term mission trips, bringing the message of hope and service to different regions and cultures.
- **Prayer and Intercession**: Join or form prayer groups dedicated to interceding for your community, seeking God's guidance and blessing on your service efforts.

Social Justice and Advocacy

- **Advocacy Groups**: Get involved with organizations that advocate for social justice, working to address issues such as poverty, inequality, and human rights.

- **Community Organizing**: Participate in community organizing efforts to address local issues, mobilizing resources and people for collective action.
- **Policy Change**: Engage in efforts to influence policy change, advocating for laws and policies that promote justice and equity.

Building Stronger Communities

- **Neighborhood Associations**: Join or start neighborhood associations to build community cohesion, address local issues, and organize events and activities.
- **Cultural Events**: Support or organize cultural events that celebrate diversity and promote understanding and unity within the community.
- **Volunteer Networks**: Create or participate in volunteer networks that connect individuals with service opportunities, fostering a culture of service and engagement.

SERVICE AND MISSION are integral to living a Christlike life. The call to serve is a universal mandate, inviting us to reflect God's love and compassion through our actions. By discerning our unique mission fields and engaging in practical ways to serve our communities, we fulfill our calling and positively impact the world. Through service, we transform the lives of those we serve and experience personal growth and spiritual fulfillment. Embracing the call to serve allows us to live out our faith in tangible and meaningful ways, embodying the love of Christ in our daily lives.

PRACTICAL APPLICATIONS

To put these principles into practice, consider the following steps:

1. **Self-Assessment:** Reflect on your skills, passions, and resources. What unique contributions can you make to your community?

2. **Research:** Identify local organizations, needs, and service opportunities. Contact community leaders and organizations to learn how you can get involved.

3. **Plan:** Develop a plan for integrating service into your life. Set realistic goals and commit to regular involvement.

4. **Act:** Begin serving in your chosen areas. Be consistent and reliable, and seek to build meaningful relationships through your service.

5. **Reflect and Adjust:** Periodically assess your involvement. Are you making a meaningful impact? Are there other areas where you can serve more effectively? Adjust your plans as needed.

BY FOLLOWING THESE STEPS, you can effectively live out your call to service and mission, making a tangible difference in your community and beyond.

CHAPTER 10
INTEGRITY AND HONESTY

The Importance of Integrity in a Christian Life

I ntegrity is one of the most fundamental virtues in a Christian's life. It is the bedrock upon which a life of faith and trustworthiness is built. Integrity means living in a manner consistent with one's values and beliefs, ensuring that our actions align with the teachings of Jesus Christ. It involves being honest, upright, and having a steadfast character regardless of external circumstances.

NUMEROUS SCRIPTURES UNDERSCORE the importance of integrity. Proverbs 11:3 states, "The integrity of the upright guides them, but their duplicity destroys the unfaithful." This verse highlights that integrity is a guiding principle, guiding believers in the right direction and protecting them from deceit and dishonesty.

INTEGRITY IS NOT ONLY ABOUT OUTWARD actions but also about inner character. It requires consistency between our internal beliefs and external behaviors. This consistency is crucial because it ensures that our faith is not merely professed but lived out in tangible ways. It is about being truthful in our dealings, keeping our promises, and being reliable in our commitments.

INTEGRITY BUILDS TRUST, a vital component in any relationship. When we are known for our integrity, people can trust that our word is reliable and that we will act ethically even when no one is watching. This trust is essential for fostering healthy relationships in our personal lives, workplaces, and communities.

LIVING with integrity also reflects our witness to the world. In Matthew 5:16, Jesus says, "Let your light shine before others, that they may see your good deeds and glorify your Father in heaven." Our integrity is a light that shines in a world often overshadowed by deceit and corruption. By living with integrity, we demonstrate the transformative power of Christ in our lives and point others to Him.

Living an Honest and Transparent Life

HONESTY IS a crucial aspect of integrity. To live an honest life means to speak the truth, act truthfully, and reject deceit in all its forms. This commitment to honesty fosters trust, builds credibility, and strengthens our relationships with others and God.

Speaking the Truth

SPEAKING the truth is the most apparent form of honesty. It involves being straightforward and transparent in our communication and avoiding lies, exaggerations, and misleading statements. Ephesians 4:25 emphasizes this principle: "Therefore each of you must put off falsehood and speak truthfully to your neighbor, for we are all members of one body." This command underscores the importance of truthfulness within the Christian community, highlighting that honesty is essential for unity and trust.

TRUTHFUL SPEECH BUILDS CREDIBILITY. When we are known for our honesty, people trust our words and believe we mean what we say. This trust is crucial in all areas of life, including personal relationships, professional interactions, and spiritual leadership. Credibility established through consistent honesty can open doors for deeper relationships and more significant influence.

. . .

Acting Truthfully

ACTING TRUTHFULLY GOES BEYOND WORDS; it encompasses our behaviors and decisions. Integrity requires that our actions align with our words and beliefs. James 2:17 teaches, "Faith by itself, if it is not accompanied by action, is dead." This verse highlights that our faith and values must be demonstrated through our actions. When we act truthfully, we live out our commitments and promises, ensuring that our behavior consistently reflects our principles.

THIS CONSISTENCY between words and actions is vital for building trust. When people see that we do what we say, they can rely on us. This reliability strengthens relationships, as others know they can depend on us to be honest and act with integrity. Whether in fulfilling promises, meeting responsibilities, or adhering to ethical standards, truthful actions affirm our commitment to honesty.

Rejecting Deceit

REJECTING DECEIT in all its forms is critical to living an honest life. Deceit can manifest in various ways, including outright lies, half-truths, manipulation, and hiding the truth. Proverbs 12:22 states, "The Lord detests lying lips, but he delights in trustworthy people." This verse indicates that deceit is abhorrent to God and that He values honesty and trustworthiness.

. . .

DECEIT UNDERMINES TRUST and damages relationships. When we deceive others, we create an environment of suspicion and insecurity. People begin to doubt our words and motives, leading to strained relationships and broken bonds. In contrast, rejecting deceit fosters an atmosphere of openness and trust, where relationships can thrive.

Honesty in Relationships

HONESTY IS the bedrock of healthy relationships. It creates a safe space where individuals can share openly and be themselves without fear of judgment or betrayal. In relationships, honesty involves clear and compassionate communication, expressing feelings and thoughts truthfully while respecting the other person's perspective.

IN MARRIAGE, honesty is essential for building intimacy and trust. Couples who communicate honestly can resolve conflicts more effectively and build a stronger, more resilient relationship. Similarly, honesty fosters loyalty and deepens the connection between friends.

Honesty with God

LIVING an honest life also means being honest with God. This involves acknowledging our sins, weaknesses, and struggles and seeking His forgiveness and guidance. Psalm 32:5 illustrates this principle: "Then I acknowledged my sin to you and did not cover up my iniquity. I said, 'I will confess my transgressions to the Lord.' And you forgave the guilt of my sin." Honest confession and repentance are vital for a genuine relationship with God.

HONESTY WITH GOD requires vulnerability and humility. It means admitting when we fall short and asking for His help to grow and improve. This openness strengthens our spiritual life, fostering a deeper connection with God and aligning our hearts with His will.

Biblical Foundations of Honesty

THE BIBLE repeatedly emphasizes the importance of honesty, underscoring it as a fundamental virtue for living a righteous life. Proverbs 12:22 states, "The Lord detests lying lips, but he delights in trustworthy people." This verse illustrates God's disdain for dishonesty and His pleasure in those who speak the truth. Honesty is not merely a personal virtue; it is a divine expectation that reflects our commitment to integrity and righteousness.

EPHESIANS 4:25 further instructs believers to "put off falsehood and speak truthfully to your neighbor, for we are all members of one body." This directive highlights that honesty is crucial for maintaining the health and unity of the Christian community. As members of one body, our words and actions impact each other. Falsehood breeds mistrust and division, whereas truthfulness fosters trust and cohesion.

HONESTY IS foundational for building trust within relationships. When we speak the truth, others know they can rely on our words, creating a safe and secure environment. This trust is essential in personal relationships and within the broader church community.

Transparency and truthfulness enable open communication, effective collaboration, and mutual support.

MOREOVER, honesty reflects God's character. God is described as a God of truth (Deuteronomy 32:4), and as His followers, we are called to emulate His nature. By living honestly, we demonstrate our alignment with His will and our desire to live in a way that honors Him.

IN PRACTICAL TERMS, honesty involves being truthful in our speech, actions, and thoughts. It means avoiding deceit, manipulation, and falsehood in all its forms. Honesty requires courage and integrity, especially when the truth is difficult or inconvenient. However, the rewards of living honestly—such as a clear conscience, strong relationships, and God's favor—far outweigh the challenges.

THE BIBLE's emphasis on honesty accentuates its importance as a virtue that pleases God and strengthens the Christian community. By committing to truthfulness, we build trust, foster unity, and reflect the character of our Creator.

The Consequences of Dishonesty

DISHONESTY HAS FAR-REACHING consequences that extend beyond immediate situations. It undermines trust, damages relationships, and tarnishes our witness as followers of Christ. When we lie or deceive, we compromise our integrity, creating a slippery slope that often leads to further dishonesty.

· · ·

Trust is fundamental to any relationship, whether personal, professional or within the church community. Dishonesty erodes this trust, making it difficult for others to believe in our words and actions. Once trust is broken, it is challenging to rebuild, often requiring significant time and effort to restore. Proverbs 19:9 warns of the severe repercussions of dishonesty: "A false witness will not go unpunished, and whoever pours out lies will perish." This scripture underscores that deceit ultimately leads to destruction regarding relationships and moral character.

Damaged relationships are another consequence of dishonesty. When we deceive others, we create a barrier between ourselves and them, leading to feelings of betrayal and hurt. If they can be repaired, these damaged relationships can take a long time to heal. The immediate benefits we might gain from deceit—such as avoiding punishment or gaining a temporary advantage—are fleeting and do not outweigh the long-term harm caused.

Moreover, dishonesty tarnishes our witness as Christians. As followers of Christ, we are called to reflect His truth and integrity in all aspects of our lives. When we engage in deceit, we contradict the values we profess to uphold and provide a poor example to others. This inconsistency can lead others to question the authenticity of our faith and diminish our ability to share the Gospel effectively.

The cycle of dishonesty can also lead to further deceit. One lie often necessitates another to cover up the first, creating a web of falsehoods that becomes increasingly difficult to maintain. This cycle not only damages our relationships but also our sense of integrity and self-worth. Living a life of deceit requires constant vigilance and fear of being discovered, leading to anxiety and stress.

THE IMMEDIATE BENEFITS of dishonesty are fleeting, while the long-term consequences can be devastating. Dishonesty undermines trust, damages relationships, and tarnishes our witness. It compromises our integrity and opens the door to further deceit, creating a cycle that is difficult to break. As Proverbs 19:9 warns, "A false witness will not go unpunished, and whoever pours out lies will perish." Committing to honesty and integrity builds trust, fosters healthy relationships, and maintains a strong and credible witness for Christ.

Practicing Honesty in Daily Life

LIVING an honest life requires a commitment to truthfulness in all our interactions. This commitment extends beyond our words to encompass our actions and thoughts. It means being genuine and sincere in everything we do, ensuring our internal beliefs align with our external behaviors. Honesty involves admitting our mistakes, taking responsibility for our actions, and resisting the temptation to exaggerate or manipulate the truth.

IN PRACTICAL TERMS, honesty involves straightforward communication. This means being transparent and truthful in what we say without resorting to half-truths, evasions, or ambiguities. When we communicate honestly, we provide accurate and complete information, which helps to build trust and understanding in our relationships. Whether speaking with friends, family, colleagues, or strangers, honesty should be our guiding principle.

. . .

HONESTY ALSO INVOLVES integrity in our work. This means ensuring we do not cut corners, misrepresent our abilities, or engage in unethical practices. For example, in a professional setting, honesty might mean accurately reporting our work hours, giving credit to others where it is due, and not falsifying records or results. By maintaining high standards of integrity, we demonstrate that we are reliable and trustworthy, which is essential for building a solid reputation.

BEING honest in our thoughts means aligning our inner attitudes with our outward expressions. It involves cultivating a mindset of truthfulness, where we seek to understand and accept reality as it is rather than as we might wish it to be. This internal honesty helps us be more authentic in our interactions with others, ensuring that our words and actions are grounded in genuine beliefs and feelings.

ONE CRITICAL ASPECT of living an honest life is admitting mistakes and taking responsibility for our actions. When we err, it is essential to acknowledge our faults and seek to make amends. This humility and willingness to accept responsibility demonstrate our commitment to honesty and build respect and trust among those we interact with. It shows that we value truth over pride and are committed to personal growth and improvement.

ANOTHER VITAL COMPONENT of honesty is avoiding the temptation to exaggerate or manipulate the truth. It can be easy to fall into the habit of embellishing stories or bending the truth to serve our purposes. However, such actions ultimately undermine our credibility and can lead to a loss of trust. By sticking to the truth, even when it is less convenient or less impressive, we maintain our integrity and build a reputation for reliability.

LIVING an honest life requires a comprehensive commitment to truthfulness in our words, actions, and thoughts. It involves straightforward communication, integrity in our work, and a mindset of internal honesty. By admitting our mistakes, taking responsibility for our actions, and avoiding exaggeration or manipulation, we build a reputation for trustworthiness and reliability. This commitment to honesty enhances our personal and professional relationships and aligns us with the ethical standards taught in the Bible and demonstrated by Jesus Christ.

Transparency and Accountability

TRANSPARENCY IS CLOSELY RELATED to honesty and is essential for living a life of integrity. Being transparent means being open and honest about our actions, decisions, and motivations. It involves a willingness to share information and to be accountable for our behavior. Transparency ensures that our lives are open books, free from hidden agendas and deceit.

IN PRACTICAL TERMS, transparency involves clear and open communication. When we make decisions, we explain our reasons and are upfront about our intentions. This openness helps others understand our actions and builds trust. For instance, in a workplace setting, transparency might involve explaining why certain decisions are made and how they align with the organization's goals. It ensures everyone is on the same page and fosters a collaborative environment.

ACCOUNTABILITY IS a crucial aspect of transparency. It means being willing to answer for our actions and to accept responsibility for our decisions. Accountability involves admitting when we are wrong and correcting our mistakes. It is about being responsible for our behavior and willing to face the consequences of our actions. In personal relationships, this might mean being honest about our feelings and actions and seeking to make amends when we have wronged someone.

IN THE CHRISTIAN COMMUNITY, accountability takes on a special significance. It can take the form of mutual support and encouragement, as well as loving correction when necessary. James 5:16 encourages believers to "confess your sins to each other and pray for each other so that you may be healed." This openness fosters a culture of trust and mutual support where integrity can thrive. When we are accountable to one another, we help each other stay on the right path and grow in our faith.

TRANSPARENCY AND ACCOUNTABILITY also involve a willingness to receive feedback and criticism. It means being open to others' perspectives and willing to learn and grow. This openness can lead to personal and spiritual growth as we become more aware of our shortcomings and work to address them.

TRANSPARENCY AND ACCOUNTABILITY are essential for living a life of integrity. Being transparent means being open and honest about our actions, decisions, and motivations, while accountability involves being willing to answer for our actions and accept responsibility for our choices. In the Christian community, these principles foster a culture of trust and mutual support where integrity can thrive. By committing to transparency and accountability, we build trust, enhance our relationships, and grow in our faith.

Overcoming Challenges to Honesty

LIVING an honest and transparent life is not always easy. In a world where dishonesty often seems to yield immediate benefits and shortcuts to success, there is significant pressure to conform to unethical practices. The fear of potential negative consequences can also make the truth seem daunting. Despite these challenges, the Bible assures us that God honors those faithful to His principles.

PROVERBS 10:9 provides a powerful promise: "Whoever walks in integrity walks securely, but whoever takes crooked paths will be found out." This verse highlights the security and peace that come from living a life of integrity. When we are honest and transparent, we do not have to worry about the consequences of deceit catching up with us. Our consistent truthfulness builds a solid foundation that cannot be easily shaken. Conversely, those who choose dishonesty and deception will eventually face the consequences of their actions.

TRUSTING in God's promises is crucial for overcoming the challenges of honesty. The Bible assures us that God is with us and will support us when we strive to live according to His will. Psalm 37:18-19 says, "The blameless spend their days under the Lord's care, and their inheritance will endure forever. In times of disaster, they will not wither; in days of famine, they will enjoy plenty." This verse rein-forces that God watches over those who live with integrity and provides for them, even in difficult times.

Relying on God's strength, we can find the courage to be honest and transparent, even when challenged. Philippians 4:13 reminds us, "I can do all this through him who gives me strength." This empowerment from God enables us to face the pressure to conform and the fear of repercussions confidently and resolvely.

Moreover, living with integrity has long-term benefits that far outweigh any short-term gains from dishonesty. It builds a reputa-tion of trustworthiness and reliability, which is invaluable in personal and professional relationships. It also fosters inner peace, as we know we live in alignment with our values and God's commandments.

Maintaining honesty and transparency might mean resisting exaggerating our achievements, admitting our mistakes at work, or being open about our struggles with friends and family. Each of these acts, though potentially tricky, strengthens our character and our witness to others.

While living an honest and transparent life can be challenging in a world that often rewards dishonesty, the Bible assures us that God honors and supports those who walk in integrity. Proverbs 10:9 reminds us that integrity leads to security and peace, while dishon-esty leads to eventual downfall. By trusting in God's promises and relying on His strength, we can overcome the challenges of honesty and live with integrity, reaping spiritual and practical rewards.

. . .

Being a Witness Through Integrity

OUR INTEGRITY IS a powerful witness to the world, demonstrating our faith's reality and the Gospel's transformative power. Integrity is about adhering to moral principles and embodying Christ's character daily. When we live with integrity, we reflect Christ's honesty, compassion, and righteousness, providing a compelling testimony to those around us.

LIVING with integrity means consistently acting in ways that are honest, ethical, and aligned with our professed beliefs. This consistency is crucial because it shows that our faith is not merely a set of abstract ideas but a living, breathing force that shapes our actions and decisions. James 2:18 emphasizes this relationship between faith and actions: "Show me your faith without deeds, and I will show you my faith by my deeds." Our integrity is the visible evidence of our inner faith, making our beliefs tangible and credible to others.

INTEGRITY ALSO BUILDS TRUST, which is essential for effective witnessing. People are likelier to listen to and be influenced by someone they perceive as trustworthy and genuine. When others see that we consistently live out our values, even in challenging circumstances, they are more likely to respect our beliefs and consider our message. This trust can open doors for meaningful conversations about faith and provide opportunities to share the Gospel.

. . .

FURTHERMORE, our integrity can inspire others to seek the same transformation. As they observe the peace, joy, and stability of living a life of integrity, they may be drawn to explore the source of that strength. In this way, our integrity becomes a beacon, guiding others toward Christ and the life-changing power of the Gospel.

THE GOSPEL's transformative power is best illustrated through the lives of believers. When we demonstrate integrity, we show that the Gospel is not just about salvation but ongoing transformation and renewal. This holistic approach to faith can resonate deeply with those seeking authenticity and purpose.

MOREOVER, integrity in our actions underscores the truth of our words. It eliminates hypocrisy, one of the most significant barriers to effective witnessing. When our actions align with our words, we present a unified and compelling testimony that underscores the authenticity of our faith.

OUR INTEGRITY SERVES as a powerful witness to the world. It demonstrates our faith's reality and the Gospel's transformative power. By living with integrity, we reflect the character of Christ, build trust, inspire others, and provide a compelling testimony to those around us. This consistency and authenticity can draw others to explore the life-changing message of Jesus Christ.

Integrity as a Reflection of Christ

JESUS IS the ultimate example of integrity. Throughout His ministry, He consistently spoke the truth, acted justly, and lived a life of perfect righteousness. From His teachings to His actions, Jesus embodied the highest standards of moral and ethical behavior, setting a benchmark for His followers to aspire to.

Jesus' commitment to truth was unwavering. He boldly proclaimed the truth of God's kingdom, even when it was unpopular or dangerous. In John 14:6, Jesus declares, "I am the way and the truth and the life." This profound statement underscores His identity as the embodiment of truth. Whether confronting the religious leaders of His time or comforting the marginalized, Jesus' words were always grounded in truth and aimed at revealing God's will and character.

Jesus' actions were equally marked by integrity. He lived out the principles He taught, ensuring no disconnect between His words and deeds. For instance, He taught about loving one's neighbor and then demonstrated this love through countless acts of compassion and healing. He emphasized justice and mercy, and His interactions with the downtrodden and outcasts vividly illustrated these principles.

One of the most poignant examples of Jesus' integrity is found in His handling of the adulterous woman in John 8:1-11. When the Pharisees brought the woman to Jesus, hoping to trap Him into making a statement they could use against Him, Jesus responded with wisdom and compassion. He acknowledged the law's requirements but highlighted the importance of mercy and forgiveness, saying, "Let any one of you without sin be the first to throw a stone at her." His response upheld the law's integrity and demonstrated profound compassion and justice.

. . .

Jesus called His followers to live with the same integrity. In His Sermon on the Mount, He instructed them to let their "yes" be "yes" and their "no" be "no" (Matthew 5:37). This directive emphasizes the importance of honesty and consistency in speech. It calls for a straightforwardness that avoids manipulation, deceit, and the need for elaborate oaths to assure others of one's truthfulness. By advocating for simple, honest communication, Jesus urged His followers to be people of their word, reliable and trustworthy in all their dealings.

Following Jesus' example of integrity means striving for a life where our actions consistently align with our professed beliefs. It involves speaking the truth even when inconvenient, acting justly, and maintaining righteousness in public and private spheres. This integrity reflects Jesus' character and glorifies God through our actions.

Moreover, integrity in our lives serves as a powerful witness to others. When we live with the same truthfulness, justice, and righteousness that characterized Jesus, we make the principles of our faith visible and credible. People are drawn to the authenticity of a life lived with integrity, which can open doors for sharing the Gospel. Our actions can inspire others to seek the source of our strength and integrity, leading them to a transformative encounter with Christ.

In addition, living with integrity builds trust within our communities. When our actions consistently reflect our words, we become known as dependable and honest individuals. This trust is crucial for building strong, healthy relationships and fostering a community where others feel safe and valued. It also provides a solid foundation for leadership within the church and other spheres of influence.

JESUS IS the ultimate example of integrity. His commitment to truth, justice, and righteousness sets His followers' standards. By speaking the truth, acting justly, and living righteously, Jesus demonstrated what it means to live with perfect integrity. He called His followers to do the same, emphasizing honesty and consistency. By following Jesus' example, we reflect His character, glorify God through our actions, and provide a powerful witness to the Gospel's transformative power.

Impact on Relationships

INTEGRITY POSITIVELY IMPACTS our relationships with others in profound ways. We build solid and healthy relationships grounded in mutual respect and trust when we are known for our honesty and trustworthiness. This trust is foundational for effective ministry and witness, as it opens doors for meaningful conversations about faith and life. Integrity fosters trust, which is the cornerstone of any strong relationship. When people know they can rely on our word and trust our intentions, they feel secure in their interactions. This security is essential for developing deep, meaningful relationships in personal friendships, family dynamics, or professional associations. Trust allows for open and honest communication, where individuals feel safe to share their thoughts, feelings, and concerns without fear of judgment or betrayal. In marriage, integrity is crucial for building and maintaining a solid bond. Spouses who are honest and transparent with each other can navigate challenges and conflicts more effectively, knowing they are committed to the truth and the relationship.

SIMILARLY, honesty fosters loyalty and deepens connections in friendships, as friends can depend on each other and feel valued for who they are. In the context of ministry and witness, integrity is especially critical. Effective ministry relies on building authentic relationships with others, which is only possible when there is trust. We earn the right to be heard when we are known for our integrity. People are likelier to listen to and engage with someone they perceive as genuine and trustworthy. This opens the door for meaningful conversations about faith, where we can fully share our beliefs and experiences. Integrity also enhances our credibility as witnesses for Christ. When our actions align with our words, we testify to the Gospel's transformative power.

PEOPLE ARE DRAWN to the authenticity of a life with integrity, which can inspire them to explore the faith that motivates them. By being honest and reliable, we demonstrate the character of Christ, making our witness more compelling and effective. Living with integrity in our relationships also equips us to handle conflicts and challenges more effectively. Conflicts can be addressed openly and constructively without defensiveness or blame when trust is established. Integrity enables us to admit our mistakes, seek forgiveness, and work toward reconciliation. This approach resolves conflicts and strengthens the relationship, showing a commitment to honesty and mutual respect. Ultimately, integrity positively impacts our relationships by fostering trust and respect, enhancing our witness, and equipping us to navigate challenges with honesty and grace.

Integrity in the Workplace

OUR INTEGRITY also extends to our professional lives, where it plays a crucial role in shaping our conduct and relationships. In the workplace, integrity involves doing our work excellently, being honest, and respecting our colleagues. Colossians 3:23-24 instructs believers to "work at it with all your heart, as working for the Lord, not for human masters, since you know you will receive an inheritance from the Lord as a reward. It is the Lord Christ you are serving." This scripture reminds us that our work is not merely for human approval but as an act of worship and service to God.

APPROACHING our work with integrity means striving for excellence in all tasks, whether large projects or minor, routine duties. Excellence reflects our commitment to doing our best and honoring God through our efforts. It involves being diligent, thorough, and conscientious in our responsibilities, ensuring that our output is of the highest quality. This dedication to excellence enhances our professional reputation and serves as a testimony to our faith.

HONESTY in our professional dealings is another critical aspect of integrity. This includes being truthful in our communications, accurately reporting our work and progress, and avoiding deceit or manipulation. Whether it involves transparent financial practices, honest reporting of time and effort, or straightforward interactions with clients and colleagues, honesty builds trust and credibility. This trust is essential for fostering a positive and ethical work environment where everyone feels valued and respected.

. . .

TREATING colleagues with respect is also a fundamental part of professional integrity. This means recognizing every individual's inherent dignity and worth, regardless of their role or position. Respectful behavior includes listening to others, valuing their contributions, and fostering an inclusive and supportive work culture. When we treat our colleagues with respect, we reflect the love and compassion of Christ, creating a workplace atmosphere that promotes collaboration and mutual support.

BY APPROACHING our work with integrity, we honor God and serve as a positive example to our coworkers. Our actions can inspire others to adopt similar standards of excellence and honesty, contributing to a culture of integrity within the organization. Additionally, our commitment to integrity can open opportunities for meaningful conversations about faith, as colleagues may be drawn to the ethical and moral way we conduct ourselves.

INTEGRITY in the workplace involves doing our work excellently, being honest in our dealings, and treating our colleagues with respect. Colossians 3:23-24 reminds us to work with all our heart, as serving the Lord. By upholding these principles, we honor God, enhance our professional reputation, and serve as a positive example to those around us.

Witnessing Through Challenges

INTEGRITY IS OFTEN TESTED in difficult times. How we respond to challenges and adversity can strengthen or weaken our witness. When we remain steadfast in our commitment to honesty and ethical behavior, even when it is costly, we provide a powerful testimony to the strength and authenticity of our faith. Difficult times often reveal a person's true character, and during these moments, the depth of our integrity is most clearly displayed.

ADVERSITY CAN TAKE MANY FORMS, such as financial struggles, workplace pressures, personal crises, or social conflicts. These situations often tempt us to take shortcuts, compromise our values, or use deceit to alleviate immediate pressures. However, succumbing to these temptations can undermine our witness and credibility. On the other hand, maintaining integrity in the face of adversity demonstrates a steadfast commitment to our principles and faith.

THE BIBLE OFFERS numerous examples of individuals who maintained their integrity under pressure. Daniel, for instance, faced the threat of death when he continued to pray to God despite a royal decree against it (Daniel 6). His unwavering faith and integrity saved him from the lions' den and was a powerful testimony to King Darius and the kingdom. Similarly, Joseph remained faithful and refused to succumb to Potiphar's wife's advances, even though his integrity led to false accusations and imprisonment (Genesis 39). In both cases, their commitment to integrity during trials showcased the strength of their faith and the power of God in their lives.

IN OUR OWN LIVES, maintaining integrity during difficult times means making decisions based on our ethical principles, even when those decisions are inconvenient or costly. It involves being honest in our communications, transparent in our actions, and consistent in our moral conduct. For example, maintaining integrity might mean resisting the temptation to engage in dishonest financial practices or fraudulent activities if we face economic hardship. It might involve standing up for what is right professionally, even if it means facing criticism or losing opportunities.

By REMAINING steadfast in our commitment to honesty and ethical behavior, we provide a powerful testimony to the authenticity of our faith. Our actions speak louder than words, and when others see us uphold our principles despite challenges, it reinforces the credibility of our witness. It shows that our faith is not just a set of beliefs but a transformative force that guides our actions and decisions, even in the most trying circumstances.

INTEGRITY IS MOST SIGNIFICANTLY TESTED in times of difficulty. By remaining committed to honesty and ethical behavior during these times, we strengthen our witness and demonstrate the strength and authenticity of our faith. Our steadfastness in adversity is a powerful testimony to the Gospel's transformative power and the reliability of our commitment to Christ.

Influencing the Community

A LIFE of integrity can significantly impact the broader community. By consistently demonstrating honesty, fairness, and ethical behavior, we influence our culture and inspire others to do the same. Integrity in our personal and professional lives sets a powerful example, showing that moral behavior is possible and beneficial. When we act with integrity, we become role models, encouraging others to uphold similar standards.

. . .

IN A WORKPLACE, for instance, an individual who practices integrity can foster a culture of trust and respect. Colleagues and subordinates often emulate the behavior of their leaders and peers. When they observe someone consistently making ethical decisions, being honest in their dealings, and treating others fairly, they are likelier to adopt these behaviors. This can lead to a more cohesive and productive work environment where everyone values and values ethical practices.

MOREOVER, the influence of integrity extends beyond immediate circles, impacting the broader society. When communities are composed of individuals who value and practice integrity, the societal fabric becomes stronger. Honest and fair dealings reduce corruption and deceit, contributing to a more just and equitable society. This creates an environment where people feel safer and more supported, knowing that others around them are committed to ethical behavior.

INTEGRITY ALSO FOSTERS compassion and empathy. When we act with integrity, we consider the impact of our actions on others, leading to more compassionate and just decisions. This can inspire others to act with kindness and fairness, creating a ripple effect that enhances the community's well-being.

FURTHERMORE, a community characterized by integrity is more likely to address and resolve social injustices. Individuals and groups who value honesty and fairness are more inclined to stand up against corruption, discrimination, and other societal issues. Their commitment to ethical behavior can drive collective efforts to create positive change, leading to a more inclusive and equitable society.

. . .

A LIFE of integrity can significantly impact the broader community by influencing the culture around us and inspiring others to demonstrate honesty, fairness, and ethical behavior. This influence contributes to a more just and compassionate society where ethical practices are valued and upheld. By consistently living with integrity, we can create a positive ripple effect that extends far beyond our immediate circles, fostering a culture of trust, respect, and empathy that benefits everyone.

Practical Steps to Strengthen Integrity

STRENGTHENING our integrity involves intentional practice and reliance on God's guidance. Here are some practical steps to help cultivate integrity in our lives:

- **Daily Reflection:** Each day, reflect on your actions and decisions and ask yourself whether they align with your values and beliefs.
- **Seek Accountability:** Surround yourself with trusted friends or mentors who can support and hold you accountable.
- **Prayer and Scripture:** Regularly seek God's guidance through prayer and study of the Bible. Ask for His help in living an integrity-filled life.
- **Honest Communication:** Commit to speaking the truth in all your interactions, even when difficult.
- **Ethical Decision-Making:** Make decisions based on moral principles rather than convenience or self-interest.

- **Transparency:** Be open and honest about your actions and motivations. This fosters trust and accountability.

INTEGRITY AND HONESTY are foundational to a Christlike life. They are essential for building trust, fostering healthy relationships, and providing a compelling witness to the world. Living an honest and transparent life reflects Christ's character and demonstrates the Gospel's transformative power. While living with integrity can be challenging, it is a vital aspect of our spiritual journey and a powerful testimony to the reality of our faith. Through daily reflection, seeking accountability, and relying on God's guidance, we can strengthen our integrity and live lives that honor God and inspire others.

~

CHAPTER 11
BOOK REVIEW REQUEST

~

Make a Difference with Your Review

Unlock the Power of Generosity

"Giving is not just about donating. It is about making a difference." - Kathy Calvin.

∼

Dear Reader,

Thank you for choosing "How to Be Christlike: A Journey of Faith, Transformation, and Legacy" by Michael Stevens. This book has guided you on your path of faith and inspired you to grow closer to Christ.

Why Your Review Matters

Your feedback is critical. By sharing your thoughts on this book, you're helping others decide if it's the right resource for them and contributing to a broader conversation about faith and transformation.

How to Leave a Review

Writing a review doesn't have to be complicated. Here are some simple steps to guide you:

1. Click **the Book's Review Link:** https://www.amazon.com/review/create-review/?ie=UTF8&channel=glance-detail&asin=B0D5HBFQG8

. . .

2. Scan the QR Code:

What to Include in Your Review

- **Personal Experience:** How did the book help you? Share specific examples.
- **Favorite Sections:** Highlight the parts of the book that were most beneficial.
- **Practical Impact:** Describe how you've applied the lessons and the changes you've seen.
- **Recommendation:** Would you recommend this book to others? Why or why not?

Example Review

"I FOUND 'HOW TO BE CHRISTLIKE' to be incredibly inspiring. The chapter on embracing forgiveness was a turning point for me. I've found a new sense of peace and connection with others by learning to forgive. The practical advice and heartfelt stories significantly impacted my faith journey. I highly recommend this book to anyone looking to deepen their relationship with Christ."

Your Impact

BY LEAVING A REVIEW, you're making a difference. Your insights can help others find spiritual guidance and encourage more open discussions about faith and personal transformation.

THANK you for taking the time to share your experience. Your voice matters; your review can help others on their faith journey.

WITH GRATITUDE,

MICHAEL Stevens

CHAPTER 12

OVERCOMING TEMPTATIONS

~

T emptation is an inevitable part of the human experience, presenting itself in various forms and stages of life. It can arise unexpectedly or be a persistent challenge, testing our resolve to live according to our values and faith. Temptation is not merely a momentary lapse in judgment; it is a significant spiritual battle that requires vigilance, strength, and a deep reliance on God's guidance.

THROUGHOUT HISTORY, even the most devout individuals have faced temptations. The Bible is replete with stories of men and women who struggled with temptation, sometimes succumbing to it and at other times overcoming it through steadfast faith and reliance on God. For instance, Adam and Eve faced the temptation to disobey God in the Garden of Eden, leading to humanity's fall. In contrast, Jesus Himself faced severe temptations in the wilderness but emerged victorious by firmly standing on the Word of God.

TEMPTATIONS OFTEN TARGET our deepest desires and weaknesses, making them particularly challenging to resist. They can manifest as the lure of material wealth, the desire for power and recognition, or the urge to engage in behaviors that provide immediate pleasure but have long-term negative consequences. These temptations can divert us from our spiritual path, leading to actions contradicting our faith and values.

RECOGNIZING the nature of temptation is the first step in overcoming it. Temptation is often subtle, presenting itself in seemingly harmless ways that can gradually lead us astray. It is essential to be aware of the various forms temptation can take and the triggers that make us vulnerable to it. This awareness allows us to anticipate and prepare for these challenges, strengthening our resolve to remain faithful.

. . .

IN THIS CHAPTER, we will delve deeply into the nature of temptation, examining its origins and the factors that make it so compelling. We will explore its psychological and spiritual aspects, understanding how it undermines our commitment to God and our values. By understanding temptation comprehensively, we can better equip ourselves to recognize and resist it.

FURTHERMORE, we will provide practical strategies to overcome temptation. These strategies will include spiritual disciplines such as prayer, meditation, and scriptural study, fortifying our minds and hearts against temptation. We will also discuss the importance of accountability and support from fellow believers and the role of self-control and avoiding situations that can lead to temptation.

ADDITIONALLY, this chapter will offer guidance on staying strong in faith during trials. Temptations often become more intense during periods of personal struggle or hardship. Maintaining our faith in such times requires a deep connection with God and a reliance on His promises. We will explore ways to cultivate this connection, including practices that help us trust God's plan and remain hopeful despite challenges.

ULTIMATELY, overcoming temptation is not about sheer willpower but aligning ourselves with God's strength and wisdom. By relying on Him and utilizing His spiritual tools, we can face temptations confidently and emerge more vital in our faith. This chapter aims to equip you with the knowledge and resources to navigate the trials of temptation, ensuring that your spiritual journey remains steadfast and true.

Recognizing Common Temptations

UNDERSTANDING AND RECOGNIZING everyday temptations is the first step in overcoming them. Temptations often target our weaknesses and exploit our desires, making knowing their forms and manifestations crucial.

Materialism and Greed

MATERIALISM AND GREED are prevalent temptations in a consumer-driven society. The constant bombardment of advertisements and societal expectations can easily lure individuals into prioritizing wealth, possessions, and status over their spiritual values. This relentless pursuit of material gain can lead to a distorted sense of self-worth and purpose, diverting attention from what truly matters.

THE DESIRE for material wealth often begins innocuously, perhaps as a means to provide for one's family or to achieve a certain level of comfort. However, this desire can quickly escalate into greed, where the accumulation of wealth and possessions becomes an end in itself. In a society that equates success with financial prosperity and social status, it's easy to fall into the trap of constantly striving for more, never feeling satisfied with what one has. This insatiable hunger for material wealth can lead to a vicious cycle of consumption and accumulation, often at the expense of one's spiritual well-being and relationships with others.

THE BIBLE explicitly warns against the dangers of materialism and greed. In 1 Timothy 6:10, it is stated, "For the love of money is a root of all kinds of evil. Some people, eager for money, have wandered from the faith and pierced themselves with many griefs." This verse highlights that it is not money itself that is inherently evil but the love of money—the overwhelming desire and pursuit of wealth—that leads to various forms of evil. This love for money can cause individuals to stray from their faith, compromising their spiritual integrity and leading to many negative consequences.

THE PURSUIT of wealth can result in numerous personal and societal issues. On an individual level, it can lead to stress, anxiety, and a never-ending cycle of dissatisfaction. People might find themselves working longer hours, neglecting family and friends, and making unethical decisions to achieve financial success. This relentless chase for more can also lead to a loss of joy and contentment, as material possessions can never truly satisfy the deeper needs of the human soul.

SOCIETALLY, materialism and greed can lead to significant inequality and injustice. When wealth and possessions are valued above all else, it can result in a culture where the rich get richer at the expense of the poor. This can create a significant divide between different socio-economic groups, leading to resentment, social unrest, and a lack of community cohesion. Furthermore, a society driven by materialism often overlooks the importance of compassion, generosity, and the well-being of others, fostering an environment where people are valued more for their wealth than their character.

THE TEACHINGS of Jesus also emphasize the futility of accumulating earthly treasures. In Matthew 6:19-21, Jesus advises, "Do not store up for yourselves treasures on earth, where moths and vermin destroy, and where thieves break in and steal. But store up for yourselves treasures in heaven, where moths and vermin do not destroy, and where thieves do not break in and steal. For where your treasure is, there your heart will be also." This passage urges believers to focus on spiritual wealth, which is eternal and imperishable, rather than on transient material possessions.

To counteract the temptations of materialism and greed, it is essential to cultivate contentment and gratitude. Recognizing and appreciating what we already have can shift our focus from what we lack to the blessings we enjoy. Philippians 4:11-13 provides a powerful reminder of this principle, where Paul writes, "I have learned to be content whatever the circumstances. I know what it is to be in need and what it is to have plenty. I have learned the secret of being content in any and every situation, whether well-fed or hungry, whether living in plenty or want. I can do all this through him who gives me strength."

Another essential strategy is to practice generosity. By giving to others, we break the hold that material possessions have on our hearts and redirect our focus toward helping those in need. Acts of generosity benefit the recipients and enrich our lives, fostering a sense of fulfillment and purpose. Jesus' teaching in Luke 12:33-34 encapsulates this: "Sell your possessions and give to the poor. Provide purses for yourselves that will not wear out, a treasure in heaven that will never fail, where no thief comes near, and no moth destroys. For where your treasure is, there your heart will be also."

. . .

MATERIALISM AND GREED are significant temptations in today's society, driven by a culture that equates success with wealth and possessions. However, the Bible warns of the dangers of prioritizing material gain over spiritual values, emphasizing that the love of money can lead to numerous evils and spiritual decline. By cultivating contentment, practicing gratitude, and embracing generosity, we can resist these temptations and focus on what truly matters, storing treasures in heaven and living a life that reflects our faith and values.

Lust and Sexual Immorality

LUST and sexual immorality are powerful temptations that can destroy relationships and lead to significant personal and spiritual harm. These temptations are pervasive in today's culture, which often normalizes and even glorifies sexual promiscuity through media, entertainment, and societal attitudes. The constant exposure to sexual content can desensitize individuals, making it increasingly difficult to maintain purity and uphold spiritual values.

SEXUAL IMMORALITY ENCOMPASSES a range of behaviors that deviate from God's design for sexuality, including adultery, fornication, pornography, and other forms of sexual misconduct. These behaviors not only violate God's commandments but also damage the integrity of relationships, erode trust, and can lead to profound emotional and psychological consequences. The Bible explicitly warns against sexual immorality in numerous passages, emphasizing the need for believers to pursue holiness and purity.

. . .

IN MATTHEW 5:28, Jesus addresses the seriousness of lust, stating, "But I tell you that anyone who looks at a woman lustfully has already committed adultery with her in his heart." This profound statement underscores that sin begins in the heart and mind, not just in outward actions. Lustful thoughts and desires are the seeds that can grow into sinful behaviors if not checked. Jesus' teaching highlights the importance of guarding our hearts and minds against impure thoughts and intentions.

THE CONSEQUENCES of giving in to lust and sexual immorality can be devastating. On a personal level, it can lead to feelings of guilt, shame, and spiritual estrangement from God. These feelings can hinder one's spiritual growth and create barriers to experiencing God's love and forgiveness. Additionally, sexual sin can lead to addictions that are difficult to break, causing ongoing struggles and pain.

RELATIONALLY, sexual immorality can shatter trust and intimacy within marriages and other relationships. Adultery, for example, is a betrayal that can irreparably damage the bond between spouses, often leading to divorce and broken families. Even in dating relationships, engaging in sexual immorality can result in emotional wounds and complications that carry into future relationships.

IN A BROADER SENSE, the normalization of sexual promiscuity in society can contribute to a culture of objectification, where individuals are valued for their physical appearance rather than their character and worth as human beings. This dehumanizing perspective can lead to a host of societal issues, including the exploitation of individuals through industries like pornography and human trafficking.

Maintaining purity in such a culture requires vigilance and self-control. It involves setting personal boundaries, being mindful of the content we consume, and actively seeking to fill our minds with pure and honorable things. Philippians 4:8 guides in this regard: "Finally, brothers and sisters, whatever is true, whatever is noble, whatever is right, whatever is pure, whatever is lovely, whatever is admirable—if anything is excellent or praiseworthy—think about such things." By focusing on positive and uplifting thoughts, we can better resist the pull of impure desires.

Self-control is a crucial aspect of resisting sexual temptation. As a fruit of the Spirit (Galatians 5:22-23), self-control is cultivated through a close relationship with God and reliance on the Holy Spirit. Developing self-control involves regular prayer, fasting, and studying scripture. These spiritual disciplines strengthen our resolve and keep our focus on God's will for our lives.

Accountability is another vital tool in maintaining purity. Having a trusted friend, mentor, or support group to share struggles with can provide encouragement, prayer, and practical advice. James 5:16 emphasizes the importance of confession and support: "Therefore confess your sins to each other and pray for each other so that you may be healed. The prayer of a righteous person is powerful and effective." An accountability partner can help keep us honest and support us to overcome temptations.

· · ·

ADDITIONALLY, avoiding situations and environments that can lead to temptation is crucial. This might mean setting boundaries on internet usage, avoiding specific social settings, or steering clear of media that glorifies sexual immorality. Proverbs 4:14-15 advises, "Do not set foot on the path of the wicked or walk in the way of evildoers. Avoid it, do not travel on it; turn from it and go on your way." Being proactive in avoiding triggers helps to minimize the risk of falling into temptation.

ULTIMATELY, maintaining purity is about striving to live in a way that honors God and aligns with His design for our lives. It requires a commitment to holiness and a willingness to make sacrifices to protect our spiritual well-being. Romans 12:1-2 urges believers to offer their bodies as living sacrifices, holy and pleasing to God, and to be transformed by renewing their minds. This transformation is a continuous process of seeking God's will and allowing His Word to shape our thoughts and actions.

LUST and sexual immorality are powerful temptations that can cause significant harm to individuals and relationships. In a culture that often normalizes these behaviors, maintaining purity requires vigilance, self-control, and a reliance on God's strength. By setting personal boundaries, seeking accountability, and focusing on pure and honorable things, believers can resist these temptations and live lives that honor God. Jesus' teachings remind us of the importance of guarding our hearts and minds, and with God's help, we can overcome these challenges and grow in our spiritual journey.

Pride and Selfishness

PRIDE AND SELFISHNESS can subtly infiltrate our hearts, leading us to prioritize our desires over the needs of others and the will of God. This temptation can manifest as a desire for recognition, power, or control. Proverbs 16:18 cautions, "Pride goes before destruction, a haughty spirit before a fall."

Anger and Bitterness

ANGER AND BITTERNESS can consume our thoughts and actions, leading to destructive behavior and fractured relationships. Holding onto grudges and allowing anger to fester can distance us from God's love and grace. Ephesians 4:31-32 advises, "Get rid of all bitterness, rage and anger, brawling and slander, along with every malice. Be kind and compassionate to one another, forgiving each other, just as in Christ God forgave you."

Deception and Dishonesty

TEMPTATIONS TO DECEIVE and be dishonest can arise in various aspects of life, from personal relationships to professional settings. Dishonesty undermines trust and integrity, leading to long-term negative consequences. Colossians 3:9-10 exhorts, "Do not lie to each other, since you have taken off your old self with its practices and have put on the new self, which is being renewed in knowledge in the image of its Creator."

Strategies to Overcome Temptations

OVERCOMING TEMPTATION REQUIRES intentional strategies and a

reliance on spiritual resources. Here are several practical approaches to help resist and overcome temptations.

Prayer and Meditation

PRAYER IS a powerful tool in resisting temptation. Jesus emphasized the importance of prayer in overcoming temptation when He instructed His disciples in Matthew 26:41, "Watch and pray so that you will not fall into temptation. The spirit is willing, but the flesh is weak." Regular prayer strengthens our connection with God and provides the spiritual fortitude to resist temptation. Meditation on scripture can also fortify our minds against temptation by filling our thoughts with God's truth.

Accountability and Support

HAVING a support system of trusted friends or mentors can provide accountability and encouragement. James 5:16 advises, "Therefore confess your sins to each other and pray for each other so that you may be healed. The prayer of a righteous person is powerful and effective." Sharing struggles with a trusted individual can offer guidance, support, and prayer, helping to resist temptation.

Avoiding Triggers

IDENTIFYING and avoiding situations or environments that trigger temptation is a practical strategy. Proverbs 4:14-15 instructs, "Do not set foot on the path of the wicked or walk in the way of evildoers. Avoid it, do not travel on it; turn from it and go on your way." By steering clear of scenarios that lead to temptation, we reduce the opportunities to succumb to it.

Scriptural Knowledge and Application

KNOWING and applying scripture is vital in resisting temptation. Jesus Himself used scripture to counter Satan's temptations in the wilderness, as recorded in Matthew 4:1-11. Memorizing and reflecting on Bible verses that address specific temptations can provide strength and clarity in moments of weakness.

Developing Self-Control

SELF-CONTROL IS a fruit of the Spirit (Galatians 5:22-23) and is essential in overcoming temptation. Practicing self-discipline in small areas of life can build resilience and help people resist more considerable temptations. Setting personal boundaries and making deliberate choices that align with our values can help maintain self-control.

Focusing on Long-Term Consequences

REFLECTING on the long-term consequences of giving in to temptation can provide a powerful deterrent. Understanding that temporary pleasure can lead to long-term pain and regret helps to reinforce the decision to resist temptation. Proverbs 14:12 warns, "There is a way that appears to be right, but in the end it leads to death."

Staying Strong in Faith During Trials

MAINTAINING faith and integrity during trials and temptations is crucial for spiritual growth and resilience. Here are some ways to stay strong in faith during challenging times.

Trusting in God's Promises

GOD'S PROMISES provide comfort and assurance during trials. Romans 8:28 reminds us, "And we know that in all things God works for the good of those who love him, who have been called according to his purpose." Trusting that God is with us and working for our good helps to sustain faith during difficult times.

Practicing Gratitude

FOCUSING on life's blessings and positive aspects can shift our perspective and strengthen our faith. Philippians 4:6-7 encourages, "Do not be anxious about anything, but in every situation, by prayer and petition, with thanksgiving, present your requests to God. And the peace of God, which transcends all understanding, will guard your hearts and minds in Christ Jesus." Practicing gratitude helps to cultivate a positive outlook and reliance on God.

Seeking Community Support

ENGAGING with a supportive faith community can provide strength and encouragement during trials. Hebrews 10:24-25 emphasizes the importance of community: "And let us consider how we may spur one another on toward love and good deeds, not giving up meeting together, as some are in the habit of doing, but encouraging one another—and all the more as you see the Day approaching." Being part of a community offers emotional and spiritual support.

Reflecting on Past Victories

REMEMBERING past experiences where God has helped us overcome challenges can boost our faith. Psalm 77:11-12 says, "I will remember the deeds of the Lord; yes, I will remember your miracles of long ago. I will consider all your works and meditate on all your mighty deeds." Reflecting on God's faithfulness in the past encourages trust in His provision for the present and future.

Engaging in Worship and Praise

WORSHIP AND PRAISE are powerful tools for staying strong in faith. They redirect our focus from our problems to God's greatness. Psalm 95:1-2 invites us, "Come, let us sing for joy to the Lord; let us shout aloud to the Rock of our salvation. Let us come before him with thanksgiving and extol him with music and song." Worship fosters a sense of connection with God and reinforces our faith.

Cultivating Patience and Endurance

PATIENCE AND ENDURANCE are essential virtues during trials. James 1:2-4 teaches, "Consider it pure joy, my brothers and sisters, whenever you face trials of many kinds because you know that testing your faith produces perseverance. Let perseverance finish its work so you may be mature and complete, not lacking anything." Developing patience helps us to trust in God's timing and purposes.

. . .

Focusing on Eternal Perspectives

KEEPING an eternal perspective helps to put current trials in context. 2 Corinthians 4:17-18 reminds us, "For our light and momentary troubles are achieving for us an eternal glory that far outweighs them all. So we fix our eyes not on what is seen, but on what is unseen since what is seen is temporary, but what is unseen is eternal." Understanding that our present sufferings are temporary and that they contribute to our eternal glory provides hope and strength.

Maintaining Spiritual Disciplines

PRACTICING spiritual disciplines such as prayer, Bible study, fasting, and worship during trials keeps us grounded in our faith. These disciplines strengthen our connection with God and provide spiritual nourishment. Ephesians 6:10-11 encourages, "Finally, be strong in the Lord and his mighty power. Put on the full armor of God so that you can take your stand against the devil's schemes."

Seeking Professional Help When Needed

SOMETIMES, professional help, such as counseling or therapy, may be necessary to navigate severe trials or temptations. Seeking help is not a sign of weakness but an acknowledgment of the need for additional support. Proverbs 11:14 states, "For lack of guidance a nation falls, but victory is won through many advisers." Professional guidance can provide tools and strategies to overcome significant challenges.

. . .

OVERCOMING TEMPTATIONS and staying strong in faith during trials are crucial components of a Christlike life. By recognizing everyday temptations, employing effective strategies to resist them, and maintaining our faith through trials, we can live with integrity and honor God in all circumstances. Temptations will always be a part of life, but with the strength and guidance of the Holy Spirit, we can overcome them and grow in our spiritual journey. Remembering that we are not alone in our struggles and that God provides the resources and support we need will empower us to live victoriously and faithfully.

CHAPTER 13

HANDLING PERSECUTION AND ADVERSITY

~

Persecution and adversity are integral parts of the Christian experience. They come in various forms and degrees of severity, but believers' responses to these challenges profoundly impact their spiritual growth and witness to the world.

This chapter will explore the nature of persecution, provide strategies for responding to adversity gracefully, and offer guidance on maintaining faith during difficult times.

Understanding Persecution

PERSECUTION IS a reality for many Christians around the world. It ranges from social ostracism and discrimination to severe violence and martyrdom. Understanding the nature and origins of persecution is crucial for preparing and responding appropriately.

Biblical Perspective on Persecution

PERSECUTION IS NOT A NEW PHENOMENON; it has been a part of the Christian experience since the early church. Jesus Himself warned His followers about the inevitability of persecution. In John 15:20, He said, "Remember what I told you: 'A servant is not greater than his master.' If they persecuted me, they will persecute you also." This statement highlights that persecution is an expected part of following Christ as believers align themselves with His teachings and mission.

Types of Persecution

PERSECUTION CAN MANIFEST **in various forms, including:**

- **Social Persecution:** This includes ridicule, exclusion, and discrimination based on faith. It often occurs in workplaces, schools, and communities where Christian beliefs are marginalized or mocked.

- **Legal Persecution:** In some regions, laws and regulations specifically target Christians, restricting their freedom to worship, evangelize, or live according to their faith.
- **Violent Persecution:** This is the most severe form, involving physical attacks, imprisonment, and even death. Many Christians around the world face such dangers daily.

Root Causes of Persecution

UNDERSTANDING the root causes of persecution can provide insights into why it happens and how to respond. Common causes include:

- **Religious Intolerance:** In societies where one religion dominates, followers of other faiths may face hostility and persecution.
- **Political Ideologies:** Some regimes view Christianity as a threat to their power and control, leading to targeted oppression.
- **Cultural Differences:** In cultures where traditional beliefs and practices are deeply ingrained, Christianity can be seen as a disruptive force, prompting backlash.

Historical Examples of Persecution

THROUGHOUT HISTORY, Christians have faced persecution in various forms. During the Roman Empire, early Christians were often martyred for their faith. Figures like Polycarp and Ignatius of

Antioch are remembered for their unwavering commitment to Christ, even in death. In more recent history, Christians in countries such as North Korea, China, and parts of the Middle East have faced severe persecution, including imprisonment and execution. These historical examples remind us of the enduring nature of persecution and the steadfast faith of those who have gone before us.

Spiritual Significance of Persecution

PERSECUTION SERVES a spiritual purpose in the life of a believer. It tests and refines faith, drawing believers closer to God and strengthening their reliance on Him. James 1:2-4 teaches, "Consider it pure joy, my brothers and sisters, whenever you face trials of many kinds because you know that testing your faith produces perseverance. Let perseverance finish its work so you may be mature and complete, not lacking anything." Persecution, while painful, can lead to spiritual maturity and deeper faith.

Global Perspective on Persecution

PERSECUTION IS NOT CONFINED to any single region but is a global issue affecting millions of Christians worldwide. Organizations such as Open Doors USA and The Voice of the Martyrs provide detailed reports and statistics on the state of Christian persecution globally. Understanding the global scale of persecution can help believers in safer environments to appreciate their freedom and support their persecuted brothers and sisters through prayer, advocacy, and aid.

Responding to Adversity with Grace

RESPONDING to adversity with grace is a hallmark of the Christian life. It involves maintaining a Christlike attitude, showing love and forgiveness, and relying on God's strength.

Emulating Christ's Example

JESUS EXEMPLIFIED how to respond to persecution and adversity with grace. He demonstrated unwavering love and forgiveness Despite mockery, betrayal, and crucifixion. In Luke 23:34, as He was being crucified, Jesus prayed, "Father, forgive them, for they do not know what they are doing." This act of grace serves as a powerful model for believers.

Practicing Forgiveness

FORGIVENESS IS a crucial aspect of responding to adversity with grace. Holding onto anger and bitterness only harms oneself and obstructs spiritual growth. Ephesians 4:31-32 instructs, "Get rid of all bitterness, rage and anger, brawling and slander, along with every malice. Be kind and compassionate to one another, forgiving each other, just as in Christ God forgave you." Forgiveness liberates the heart and allows for healing and reconciliation.

Showing Love to Persecutors

JESUS TAUGHT His followers to love their enemies and pray for those persecuting them (Matthew 5:44). This radical love transcends human inclinations and reflects the Gospel's transformative power. By showing love and kindness to persecutors, believers can demonstrate the love of Christ and potentially soften the hearts of those who oppose them.

Relying on God's Strength

ADVERSITY OFTEN REVEALS the limits of human strength and the necessity of relying on God. Philippians 4:13 reassures us, "I can do all this through him who gives me strength." In times of persecution and hardship, praying to God and seeking His guidance provides the strength to endure and remain faithful.

Maintaining Joy and Hope

MAINTAINING joy and hope amidst adversity is possible through a deep connection with God. Romans 12:12 encourages believers to "be joyful in hope, patient in affliction, faithful in prayer." Joy comes from the assurance of God's presence and the hope of His promises. Focusing on eternal perspectives helps sustain joy even in the face of suffering.

Seeking Community Support

A SUPPORTIVE FAITH community is vital in helping believers respond to adversity with grace. Hebrews 10:24-25 highlights the importance of mutual encouragement: "And let us consider how we may spur one another on toward love and good deeds, not giving up meeting together, as some are in the habit of doing, but encouraging one another—and all the more as you see the Day approaching." Community involvement provides emotional and spiritual support, prayer, and practical help.

. . .

Developing Resilience Through Adversity

RESILIENCE IS the capacity to recover quickly from difficulties and is essential for navigating persecution and adversity. Developing resilience involves:

- **Mental Fortitude:** Cultivating a mindset that embraces challenges as opportunities for growth rather than threats.
- **Emotional Regulation:** Learning to manage and express emotions healthily, reducing stress, and maintaining mental clarity.
- **Spiritual Anchoring:** Deepening one's relationship with God to provide a stable foundation during turbulent times.

LEARNING from Biblical Figures

The Bible is filled with examples of individuals who faced persecution and adversity with grace and resilience. Studying their lives can provide inspiration and guidance. For example:

- **Joseph:** Despite being sold into slavery by his brothers and later imprisoned unjustly, Joseph remained faithful to God. His Genesis 37-50 story demonstrates how God can turn adversity into a blessing.
- **Daniel:** Daniel's unwavering faith in God, despite being thrown into the lion's den, is a powerful testament to the strength of faith in the face of persecution (Daniel 6).

- **Paul:** The Apostle Paul endured numerous hardships, including imprisonment, beatings, and shipwrecks. His letters, especially 2 Corinthians 11:23-28, reveal his resilience and unwavering commitment to his mission.

Maintaining Faith in Difficult Times

MAINTAINING faith during difficult times requires intentional practices and a deep reliance on God. Here are some strategies for sustaining faith through adversity.

Grounding in Scripture

THE BIBLE IS a source of strength and encouragement during trials. Scriptures remind believers of God's promises, faithfulness, and sovereignty. Psalm 119:105 declares, "Your word is a lamp for my feet, a light on my path." Regular Bible study and meditation help anchor faith and provide guidance.

Persistent Prayer

PRAYER IS a lifeline in times of adversity. It connects believers to God, allowing them to express their fears, hopes, and needs. Philippians 4:6-7 advises, "Do not be anxious about anything, but in every situation, by prayer and petition, with thanksgiving, present your requests to God. And the peace of God, which transcends all understanding, will guard your hearts and minds in Christ Jesus." Persistent prayer fosters peace and trust in God's provision.

Worship and Praise

WORSHIP SHIFTS FOCUS from problems to God's greatness and goodness. Acts of worship, whether through singing, praising, or other forms, remind believers of God's sovereignty and ability to overcome any challenge. Psalm 100:2-4 encourages, "Worship the Lord with gladness; come before him with joyful songs. Know that the Lord is God. He made us, and we are his; we are his people, the sheep of his pasture. Enter his gates with thanksgiving and his courts with praise; give thanks to him and praise his name."

Cultivating Spiritual Disciplines

MAINTAINING spiritual disciplines such as fasting, service, and solitude can strengthen faith during trials. These practices foster a deeper relationship with God and provide spiritual nourishment. Ephesians 6:10-11 emphasizes the importance of spiritual preparation: "Finally, be strong in the Lord and his mighty power. Put on the full armor of God so that you can take your stand against the devil's schemes."

Reflecting on God's Faithfulness

REMEMBERING past experiences of God's faithfulness can bolster faith. Reflecting on how God has previously provided, protected, and guided through difficult times encourages trust in His ongoing faithfulness. Lamentations 3:22-23 assures, "Because of the Lord's great love we are not consumed, for his compassions never fail. They are new every morning; great is your faithfulness."

Embracing Community Support

ENGAGING with a faith community offers crucial support during trials. Fellow believers can provide encouragement, prayer, and practical assistance. Ecclesiastes 4:9-10 highlights the strength found in the community: "Two are better than one, because they have a good return for their labor: If either of them falls, one can help the other up. But pity anyone who falls and has no one to help them up."

Maintaining a Heavenly Perspective

FOCUSING on the eternal perspective helps believers endure temporary trials. Colossians 3:1-2 advises, "Since you have been raised with Christ, set your hearts on things above, where Christ is, seated at the right hand of God. Set your minds on things above, not on earthly things." Understanding that earthly sufferings are temporary and eternal glory awaits provides hope and resilience.

Professional Support When Needed

IN SEVERE CASES of persecution and adversity, professional support such as counseling or therapy may be necessary. Seeking help is a practical step toward healing and resilience. Proverbs 11:14 underscores the value of wise counsel: "For lack of guidance a nation falls, but victory is won through many advisers." Professional support can offer tools and strategies to navigate complex challenges.

Engaging in Continuous Learning

CONTINUOUS LEARNING and personal development can fortify faith and provide new perspectives on handling adversity. This can include:

- **Reading:** Engaging with books, articles, and other resources that offer insights into faith, resilience, and overcoming adversity.
- **Seminars and Workshops:** Participating in seminars and workshops focused on spiritual growth, resilience, and coping strategies.
- **Mentorship:** Seeking guidance from more experienced believers who can provide wisdom and support.

Utilizing Creative Expression

CREATIVE EXPRESSION CAN BE a powerful outlet for processing emotions and finding solace during difficult times. This can include:

- **Writing:** Journaling thoughts and prayers can provide clarity and emotional release.
- **Art:** Engaging in visual arts, music, or dance can offer a therapeutic way to express feelings and connect with God.
- **Storytelling:** Sharing personal stories of faith and resilience can inspire others and reinforce one's beliefs.

Finding Strength in Nature

NATURE CAN BE a source of peace and inspiration, connecting to God's creation. Activities such as hiking, gardening, or simply spending time outdoors can:

- **Reduce Stress:** Nature has a calming effect, reducing stress and anxiety.
- **Enhance Spiritual Connection:** Observing the beauty and intricacy of creation can deepen one's sense of wonder and connection to the Creator.
- **Provide Perspective:** Nature's cycles of growth and renewal can remind us of God's faithfulness and the promise of new beginnings.

DEVELOPING a Routine of Gratitude

Gratitude is a powerful practice that can shift focus from what is lacking to what is present. Developing a routine of gratitude involves:

- **Daily Reflections:** Take time each day to reflect on and give thanks for blessings and positive experiences.
- **Gratitude Journals:** Keeping a journal documenting things one is grateful for can reinforce positive thinking and resilience.
- **Expressing Thanks:** Expressing gratitude fosters positive relationships and a supportive community.

HANDLING persecution and adversity with grace and faith is a testament to the Gospel's transformative power. Believers can navigate these challenges with strength and integrity by understanding the nature of persecution, responding with love and forgiveness, and maintaining faith through intentional spiritual practices. Persecution and adversity, while painful, offer opportunities for spiritual growth and a deeper reliance on God. Through His strength and guidance, believers can emerge from these trials with a stronger, more resilient faith, serving as powerful witnesses to the world of God's love and faithfulness.

CHAPTER 14

GROWTH THROUGH TRIALS

～

The journey of faith is often marked by trials and tribulations that test our resolve and shape our character. While suffering and challenges can be daunting, they provide unique spiritual growth and transformation opportunities. This chapter explores the role of suffering in spiritual growth, the lessons we can learn from life's challenges, and how embracing trials can lead to profound personal and spiritual development.

The Role of Suffering in Spiritual Growth

SUFFERING IS an inevitable part of the human experience and plays a significant role in developing our spiritual lives. Throughout history, believers have faced various forms of suffering, from physical pain and illness to emotional distress and persecution. While suffering is often seen as a negative experience, it can also be a powerful catalyst for growth and transformation.

Biblical Perspective on Suffering

THE BIBLE OFFERS numerous insights into the purpose and value of suffering. In Romans 5:3-5, the Apostle Paul writes, "Not only so, but we also glory in our sufferings, because we know that suffering produces perseverance; perseverance, character; and character, hope. And hope does not put us to shame because God's love has been poured out into our hearts through the Holy Spirit, who has been given to us." This passage highlights the transformative power of suffering, leading to perseverance, character development, and hope.

Refining Faith Through Suffering

SUFFERING serves as a refining process for our faith. Just as gold is purified through fire, our faith is strengthened and purified through the trials we endure. 1 Peter 1:6-7 states, "In all this you greatly rejoice, though now for a little while you may have had to suffer grief in all kinds of trials. These have come so that the proven genuineness of your faith—of greater worth than gold, which perishes even though refined by fire—may result in praise, glory, and honor when Jesus Christ is revealed." Trials test our faith's authenticity and help us develop a deeper, more resilient trust in God.

Drawing Closer to God

Suffering often leads us to seek a closer relationship with God. In times of pain and difficulty, we are reminded of our dependence on Him and our need for His guidance and comfort. Psalm 34:18 assures us, "The Lord is close to the brokenhearted and saves those who are crushed in spirit." We profoundly experience God's presence through suffering, deepening our intimacy with Him.

Building Empathy and Compassion

Experiencing suffering helps us to develop greater empathy and compassion for others. When we have walked through our trials, we are better equipped to understand and support those who are facing similar challenges. 2 Corinthians 1:3-4 explains, "Praise be to the God and Father of our Lord Jesus Christ, the Father of compassion and the God of all comfort, who comforts us in all our troubles so that we can comfort those in any trouble with the comfort we receive from God." Our suffering can become a source of comfort and encouragement for others.

Learning and Growing from Life's Challenges

Life's challenges offer valuable lessons that can shape our character and deepen our faith. We can grow in wisdom and maturity by approaching these challenges with an open heart and a willingness to learn.

Embracing a Growth Mindset

A growth mindset is the belief that our abilities and intelligence can be developed through dedication and hard work. This mindset encourages us to view challenges as opportunities for growth rather than obstacles to be avoided. James 1:2-4 advises, "Consider it pure joy, my brothers and sisters, whenever you face trials of many kinds because you know that testing your faith produces perseverance. Let perseverance finish its work so you may be mature and complete, not lacking anything." We can approach life's challenges with optimism and resilience by embracing a growth mindset.

Identifying Personal Strengths and Weaknesses

Challenges often reveal our strengths and weaknesses, providing valuable insights into areas where we can grow. By reflecting on our responses to difficult situations, we can identify the qualities that serve us well and those that need improvement. This self-awareness allows us to develop a more balanced and practical approach to life.

Developing Resilience

Resilience is the ability to bounce back from adversity and continue moving forward. It is crucial for navigating life's challenges and growing through trials. Romans 8:28 reminds us, "And we know that in all things God works for the good of those who love him, who have been called according to his purpose." By trusting in God's plan and cultivating resilience, we can overcome setbacks and emerge stronger.

Learning Patience and Perseverance

PATIENCE AND PERSEVERANCE are essential virtues for enduring and growing through trials. These qualities enable us to remain steadfast and committed, even when the journey is difficult. Hebrews 12:1-2 encourages us, "Therefore since such a great cloud of witnesses surrounds us, let us throw off everything that hinders and the sin that so easily entangles. And let us run with perseverance the race marked out for us, fixing our eyes on Jesus, the pioneer and perfecter of faith." By focusing on Jesus and relying on His strength, we can develop the patience and perseverance to navigate life's challenges.

Gaining Perspective

CHALLENGES OFTEN PROVIDE us with a broader perspective on life. They help us to recognize what is truly important and to prioritize our values and goals accordingly. 2 Corinthians 4:17-18 offers a perspective on suffering: "For our light and momentary troubles are achieving for us an eternal glory that far outweighs them all. So we fix our eyes not on what is seen, but on what is unseen since what is seen is temporary, but what is unseen is eternal." By focusing on the eternal, we can better understand the purpose and value of our trials.

Embracing Trials as Opportunities for Growth

EMBRACING trials as opportunities for growth requires a shift in perspective and a willingness to trust in God's plan. We can transform adversity into a source of strength and wisdom by viewing challenges as catalysts for personal and spiritual development.

Trusting in God's Sovereignty

TRUSTING in God's sovereignty means believing He is in control and has a purpose for our suffering. Romans 8:18 reassures us, "I consider that our present sufferings are not worth comparing with the glory that will be revealed in us." We can find peace and hope amid our trials by trusting God's plan.

Seeing Challenges as Divine Appointments

RATHER THAN VIEWING challenges as obstacles, we can see them as divine appointments—opportunities arranged by God to help us grow and fulfill His purposes. Proverbs 3:5-6 advises, "Trust in the Lord with all your heart and lean not on your understanding; in all your ways submit to him, and he will make your paths straight." By submitting to God's guidance, we can navigate challenges with confidence and purpose.

Cultivating a Spirit of Gratitude

GRATITUDE TRANSFORMS our perspective on trials, allowing us to see the blessings and opportunities within them. 1 Thessalonians 5:18 instructs, "Give thanks in all circumstances; for this is God's will for you in Christ Jesus." By cultivating a spirit of gratitude, we can embrace trials with a positive and hopeful attitude.

Finding Strength in Community

THE COMMUNITY PROVIDES SUPPORT, encouragement, and accountability during times of trial. We can draw strength from their faith and experiences by surrounding ourselves with fellow believers. Galatians 6:2 encourages us, "Carry each other's burdens, and in this way, you will fulfill the law of Christ." By supporting one another, we can navigate trials together and grow in unity and love.

Engaging in Continuous Prayer

PRAYER IS a powerful tool for finding strength and guidance during trials. It connects us with God and allows us to seek His wisdom and comfort. Philippians 4:6-7 advises, "Do not be anxious about anything, but in every situation, by prayer and petition, with thanksgiving, present your requests to God. And the peace of God, which transcends all understanding, will guard your hearts and minds in Christ Jesus." We can find peace and clarity amidst life's challenges through prayer.

Reflecting on Past Victories

REFLECTING on past victories reminds us of God's faithfulness and the strength we have gained through previous trials. By recalling how God has brought us through difficult times, we can find the courage and faith to face current challenges. Deuteronomy 31:8 reassures us, "The Lord himself goes before you and will be with you; he will never leave or forsake you. Do not be afraid; do not be discouraged." We can trust His continued presence and support by remembering God's faithfulness.

Seeking God's Purpose in Trials

Seeking God's purpose in trials involves asking Him to reveal the lessons and growth opportunities within our challenges. Romans 12:12 encourages us to "be joyful in hope, patient in affliction, faithful in prayer." We can discover the purpose and meaning behind our trials by remaining open to God's guidance and seeking His will.

Embracing Vulnerability

Embracing vulnerability allows us to acknowledge our weaknesses and seek support from others. It involves being honest about our struggles and allowing others to walk alongside us in our journey. 2 Corinthians 12:9-10 reminds us, "But he said to me, 'My grace is sufficient for you, for my power is made perfect in weakness.' Therefore, I will boast all the more gladly about my weaknesses so that Christ's power may rest on me. That is why, for Christ's sake, I delight in weaknesses, insults, hardships, persecutions, and difficulties. For when I am weak, then I am strong." By embracing vulnerability, we can experience God's strength in our weakness.

Practical Steps for Embracing Trials

Adopting practical steps that foster resilience, faith, and personal development is essential for effectively embracing and growing through trials.

Developing a Daily Devotional Practice

A DAILY DEVOTIONAL practice helps to anchor our faith and provides a foundation for spiritual growth. This practice can include reading Scripture, praying, journaling, and reflecting on God's word. By setting aside time each day for devotion, we can draw closer to God and gain the strength to navigate trials.

Setting Goals for Personal Growth

SETTING goals for personal growth allows us to approach trials with a sense of purpose and direction. These goals include developing virtues, improving relationships, or achieving personal milestones. By setting and pursuing these goals, we can transform trials into opportunities for growth and achievement.

Building a Support Network

A STRONG SUPPORT network provides encouragement, guidance, and accountability during times of trial. This network can include family, friends, mentors, and faith communities. Building and maintaining these relationships allows us to draw strength and support from others as we navigate challenges.

Practicing Self-Care

SELF-CARE IS essential for maintaining physical, emotional, and spiritual well-being during trials. This practice can include exercise, proper nutrition, rest, and engaging in hobbies and activities that bring joy and relaxation. By prioritizing self-care, we can build resilience and maintain the energy needed to face challenges.

Engaging in Acts of Service

SERVING others can provide a sense of purpose and fulfillment during times of trial. Acts of service can include volunteering, helping those in need, and supporting fellow believers. By focusing on the needs of others, we can shift our perspective from our struggles and find joy in making a positive impact.

Continuing Education and Personal Development

EDUCATION and personal development can help us grow in knowledge, skills, and wisdom. This pursuit can include formal education, online courses, workshops, and reading. We can develop the tools and insights needed to navigate trials and achieve personal growth by continually learning and growing.

Maintaining a Positive Attitude

A POSITIVE ATTITUDE can significantly impact our ability to embrace and grow through trials. By focusing on the positive aspects of our situation and maintaining an optimistic outlook, we can cultivate resilience and hope. Philippians 4:8 advises, "Finally, brothers and sisters, whatever is true, whatever is noble, whatever is right, whatever is pure, whatever is lovely, whatever is admirable—if anything is excellent or praiseworthy—think about such things." Focusing on the positive can transform our perspective on trials and find strength in adversity.

GROWTH THROUGH TRIALS is a testament to the transformative power of God's grace and the resilience of the human spirit. By understanding the role of suffering in spiritual growth, learning from life's challenges, and embracing trials as opportunities for development, we can navigate adversity with strength and purpose. Through intentional practices, a supportive community, and a deep reliance on God, we can emerge from trials with a stronger, more resilient faith, ready to face whatever challenges lie ahead.

CHAPTER 15
SPREADING THE GOSPEL

~

The call to spread the Gospel is at the heart of the Christian faith. As followers of Christ, we are entrusted with sharing His love, grace, and truth with the world. This chapter explores the significance of the Great Commission, effective ways to share your faith, and how to live as an example of Christ's love in everyday life.

The Great Commission

THE GREAT COMMISSION is the mandate given by Jesus to His disciples to spread the Gospel to all nations. It is a call to evangelize, disciple, and baptize in the name of the Father, the Son, and the Holy Spirit. This mission is not limited to a select few but is a universal charge to all believers.

Biblical Foundation

THE GREAT COMMISSION is rooted in several key passages of Scripture. In Matthew 28:18-20, Jesus commands His disciples, saying, "All authority in heaven and on earth has been given to me. Therefore, go and make disciples of all nations, baptizing them in the name of the Father, the Son, and the Holy Spirit and teaching them to obey everything I have commanded. And surely I am with you to the very end of the age." This passage emphasizes the authority of Christ, the call to disciple all nations, and the promise of His continual presence.

Historical Context

UNDERSTANDING the historical context of the Great Commission provides deeper insight into its significance. Jesus issued this command after His resurrection and before His ascension into heaven. At this pivotal moment, He imparted a mission that would define the purpose and direction of His followers. The early church took this commission seriously, spreading the Gospel throughout the Roman Empire and beyond despite facing persecution and hardship.

The Scope of the Great Commission

THE GREAT COMMISSION extends to all corners of the earth, transcending cultural, linguistic, and geographical boundaries. Acts 1:8 reinforces this global mission: "But you will receive power when the Holy Spirit comes on you, and you will be my witnesses in Jerusalem, and in all Judea and Samaria, and to the ends of the earth." This passage outlines the expansive reach of the Gospel, starting locally and extending globally.

The Urgency of the Mission

THE URGENCY of spreading the Gospel is underscored by the reality of eternity and the need for all people to hear the message of salvation. Romans 10:14-15 emphasizes the importance of evangelism: "How, then, can they call on the one they have not believed in? And how can they believe in the one whom they have not heard? And how can they hear without someone preaching to them? And how can anyone preach unless they are sent? As it is written: 'How beautiful are the feet of those who bring good news!'" The mission to spread the Gospel is urgent and beautiful, as it brings the hope of salvation to those who need it.

Effective Ways to Share Your Faith

SHARING your faith effectively requires a combination of boldness, wisdom, and sensitivity. It involves understanding the message of the Gospel, building relationships, and communicating with clarity and compassion.

Understanding the Gospel Message

TO SHARE THE GOSPEL EFFECTIVELY, it is essential to understand its core message clearly. The Gospel is the good news of Jesus Christ—His life, death, resurrection, and the offer of salvation to all who believe. Key elements of the Gospel include:

- **God's Love:** John 3:16 encapsulates the essence of the Gospel: "For God so loved the world that he gave his one and only Son, that whoever believes in him shall not perish but have eternal life."
- **Human Sinfulness:** Romans 3:23 highlights the need for salvation: "For all have sinned and fall short of the glory of God."
- **Christ's Sacrifice:** Romans 5:8 demonstrates God's love through Christ's sacrifice: "But God demonstrates his love for us in this: While we were still sinners, Christ died for us."
- **Salvation by Faith:** Ephesians 2:8-9 emphasizes salvation by grace through faith: "For it is by grace you have been saved, through faith—and this is not from yourselves, it is the gift of God—not by works so that no one can boast."

Building Relationships

EFFECTIVE EVANGELISM often begins with building genuine relationships. Connecting with others personally creates opportunities to share our faith naturally and meaningfully. Critical principles for building relationships include:

- **Listening:** Listening to others' stories, struggles, and questions demonstrates care and respect.
- **Empathy:** Showing empathy and understanding helps to build trust and opens doors for deeper conversations.
- **Service:** Serving others in practical ways reflects Christ's love and creates opportunities to share the Gospel.

Communicating with Clarity and Compassion

WHEN SHARING THE GOSPEL, it is essential to communicate with clarity and compassion. This involves:

- **Being Clear and Concise:** Clearly articulate the critical points of the Gospel without overwhelming the listener with too much information at once.
- **Using Simple Language:** Avoid theological jargon and use simple language that is easy to understand.
- **Sharing Personal Testimony:** Sharing your own story of faith can make the message more relatable and impactful.
- **Showing Respect:** Respect the listener's beliefs and perspectives, and approach the conversation humbly and kindly.

. . .

Utilizing Various Platforms

IN TODAY'S DIGITAL AGE, numerous platforms are available for sharing the Gospel. These include:

- **Social Media:** Using platforms like Facebook, Instagram, and Twitter to share Scripture, testimonies, and encouraging messages.
- **Blogs and Websites:** Writing blog posts or creating a personal website to share the Gospel and provide resources for seekers.
- **Podcasts and Videos:** Creating podcasts or videos to discuss faith topics and share the message of Christ.
- **Public Speaking:** Engaging in public speaking opportunities, such as church events, conferences, and community gatherings, to share the Gospel.

Engaging in Apologetics

APOLOGETICS IS the practice of defending the faith through reasoned arguments and evidence. Engaging in apologetics involves:

- **Understanding Common Questions:** Familiarize yourself with common questions and objections to Christianity, such as the problem of evil, the reliability of the Bible, and the evidence for the resurrection.
- **Providing Reasoned Responses:** Respond thoughtfully and well-reasoned to these questions, drawing from Scripture, historical evidence, and logical arguments.

- **Showing Respect for Different Views:** Approach apologetic conversations with respect and a willingness to listen to different perspectives.

Adapting Your Approach to Different Contexts

DIFFERENT CULTURAL AND social contexts require different approaches to sharing the Gospel. Understanding and respecting these contexts can enhance the effectiveness of your evangelism efforts. This involves:

- **Cultural Sensitivity:** Recognizing and respecting cultural norms, values, and practices.
- **Contextualization:** Presenting the Gospel in a relevant and understandable way to the specific audience.
- **Building Trust:** Establishing trust and credibility within the community before sharing the Gospel message.

Collaborating with Other Believers

COLLABORATING with other believers can amplify your evangelism efforts. Working together in unity and love demonstrates the power of the Gospel and provides a more vital witness to the world. This can include:

- **Team Evangelism:** Partnering with others to share the Gospel in various settings, such as community events, mission trips, and outreach programs.

- **Supporting Local Churches:** Collaborating with local churches to support their evangelism efforts and build relationships within the community.
- **Praying Together:** Engaging in collective prayer for guidance, boldness, and opportunities to share the Gospel.

Being Persistent and Patient

SHARING the Gospel often requires persistence and patience. Not everyone will respond immediately or positively to the message. It is essential to:

- **Be Persistent:** Continue to share the Gospel with love and compassion, even when faced with resistance or indifference.
- **Be Patient:** Understand that transformation and acceptance of the Gospel can take time. Trust in God's timing and continue to pray for those you witness.
- **Celebrate Small Victories:** Celebrate small steps of faith and progress, and trust that God is at work even when the results are not immediately visible.

Living as an Example of Christ's Love

ONE OF THE most powerful ways to spread the Gospel is by living as an example of Christ's love. Our actions, attitudes, and relationships can either attract people to Christ or turn them away.

Embodying Christ's love daily, we can be a living testimony to the Gospel's transformative power.

Demonstrating Christlike Love

CHRISTLIKE LOVE IS CHARACTERIZED by selflessness, compassion, and sacrificial service. Critical aspects of demonstrating this love include:

- **Selflessness:** Putting the needs and interests of others before our own, as exemplified by Jesus in Philippians 2:3-4: "Do nothing out of selfish ambition or vain conceit. Rather, in humility, value others above yourselves, not looking to your interests but each of you to the interests of the others."
- **Compassion shows** genuine care and concern for others, as Jesus did in Matthew 9:36: "When he saw the crowds, he had compassion on them, because they were harassed and helpless, like sheep without a shepherd."
- **Service:** Serving others with humility and love, following Jesus' example in John 13:14-15: "Now that I, your Lord and Teacher, have washed your feet, you also should wash one another's feet. I have set an example that you should do as I have done for you."

Living with Integrity

INTEGRITY IS essential for living as an example of Christ's love. It involves honesty, trustworthiness, and consistency in our actions and words. Proverbs 11:3 emphasizes the importance of integrity: "The integrity of the upright guides them, but their duplicity destroys the unfaithful." Living with integrity reflects Christ's character and builds trust with others.

Practicing Forgiveness and Reconciliation

Forgiveness and reconciliation are core components of the Gospel message. By practicing these virtues in our relationships, we demonstrate the power of God's grace and mercy. Colossians 3:13 instructs, "Bear with each other and forgive one another if you have a grievance against someone. Forgive as the Lord forgave you." By forgiving others and seeking reconciliation, we model the forgiveness we have received from Christ.

Cultivating a Spirit of Humility

Humility is a crucial characteristic of Christlike living. It involves recognizing our dependence on God and valuing others above ourselves. Philippians 2:5-7 encourages us to adopt the mindset of Christ: "In your relationships with one another, have the same mindset as Christ Jesus: Who, being in very nature God, did not consider equality with God something to be used to his advantage; rather, he made himself nothing by taking the very nature of a servant, being made in human likeness." By cultivating a spirit of humility, we reflect the character of Christ and draw others to Him.

Building Authentic Relationships

AUTHENTIC RELATIONSHIPS ARE BUILT on trust, transparency, and mutual respect. Investing in these relationships creates opportunities to share our faith and demonstrate Christ's love. Critical principles for building authentic relationships include:

- **Honesty:** Being truthful and transparent in our interactions.
- **Consistency:** Being reliable and consistent in our actions and words.
- **Empathy:** Showing empathy and understanding for others' experiences and perspectives.
- **Support:** Providing support and encouragement in times of need.

Engaging in Community Involvement

ACTIVE INVOLVEMENT in the community provides opportunities to build relationships and share the Gospel through actions and service. This can include:

- **Volunteering:** Participating in community service projects and local charities.
- **Joining Local Groups:** Getting involved in local clubs, organizations, or sports teams.
- **Attending Community Events:** Attending community gatherings, festivals, and events.

Creating a Welcoming Environment

CREATING a welcoming and inclusive environment in our homes, churches, and communities can open doors for sharing the Gospel. This involves:

- **Hospitality:** Opening our homes and hearts to others, offering hospitality and kindness.
- **Inclusivity:** Ensuring that everyone feels welcome and valued, regardless of their background or beliefs.
- **Encouragement:** Providing a supportive and encouraging atmosphere where people feel safe to explore and ask questions about faith.

Practicing Gratitude

GRATITUDE IS a powerful witness to God's goodness and faithfulness. By expressing gratitude daily, we reflect the joy and contentment of a relationship with Christ. 1 Thessalonians 5:18 encourages, "Give thanks in all circumstances; for this is God's will for you in Christ Jesus." Practicing gratitude can inspire others to seek the source of our joy and thankfulness.

Modeling Faithfulness

FAITHFULNESS IN OUR COMMITMENTS, relationships, and responsibilities demonstrates the reliability and trustworthiness of Christ. We build a strong testimony of God's faithfulness by being faithful in the small things. Luke 16:10 reminds us, "Whoever can be trusted with very little can also be trusted with much, and whoever is dishonest with very little will also be dishonest with much."

Modeling faithfulness in all areas of our lives reflects the character of Christ and builds credibility with others.

Living a Life of Prayer

A PRAYER LIFE is essential for maintaining a close relationship with God and seeking His guidance in all aspects of life. By prioritizing prayer, we demonstrate our dependence on God and commitment to His will. 1 Thessalonians 5:16-18 instructs, "Rejoice always, pray continually, give thanks in all circumstances; for this is God's will for you in Christ Jesus." Consistent prayer strengthens our faith and sets an example for others to follow.

Displaying Joy and Peace

JOY AND PEACE are fruits of the Spirit, evident in the lives of believers who trust in God. By displaying joy and peace, even under challenging circumstances, we testify to the sustaining power of God's presence. Philippians 4:4-7 encourages, "Rejoice in the Lord always. I will repeat it: Rejoice! Let your gentleness be evident to all. The Lord is near. Do not be anxious about anything, but in every situation, by prayer and petition, with thanksgiving, present your requests to God. And the peace of God, which transcends all understanding, will guard your hearts and minds in Christ Jesus." Living with joy and peace can attract others to our hope in Christ.

Exercising Patience and Kindness

PATIENCE AND KINDNESS are essential for building meaningful relationships and sharing the Gospel. By exercising these virtues, we reflect the character of Christ and create a welcoming environment for others. Colossians 3:12-13 advises, "Therefore, as God's chosen people, holy and dearly loved, clothe yourselves with compassion, kindness, humility, gentleness, and patience. Bear with each other and forgive one another if any of you has a grievance against someone. Forgive as the Lord forgave you." Demonstrating patience and kindness can open hearts and minds to the message of the Gospel.

Engaging in Continuous Learning and Growth

CONTINUOUS LEARNING and growth are vital for effective evangelism and personal development. We can better understand and articulate our faith by seeking knowledge and wisdom. Proverbs 18:15 states, "The heart of the discerning acquires knowledge, for the ears of the wise seek it out." Engaging in Bible study, attending seminars, and reading books on theology and apologetics can equip us to share the Gospel more effectively.

Fostering a Spirit of Generosity

GENEROSITY REFLECTS the heart of God and can be a powerful witness to His love and provision. We demonstrate the Gospel's transformative power by generously giving our time, resources, and talents. 2 Corinthians 9:6-7 encourages, "Remember this: Whoever sows sparingly will also reap sparingly, and whoever sows generously will also reap generously. Each of you should give what you have decided to give, not reluctantly or under compulsion, for God loves a cheerful giver." Generosity can touch lives and open doors for sharing the Gospel.

. . .

SPREADING the Gospel is a vital and urgent mission for all believers. By understanding the Great Commission, utilizing effective ways to share our faith, and living as examples of Christ's love, we can fulfill this mission with passion and purpose. Through intentional relationships, clear communication, and Christlike living, we can share the hope and truth of the Gospel with a world in need.

CHAPTER 16

BOOK REVIEW REQUEST

~

Make a Difference with Your Review

Unlock the Power of Generosity

"Giving is not just about donating. It is about making a difference." - Kathy Calvin.

∽

DEAR READER,

Thank you for choosing "How to Be Christlike: A Journey of Faith, Transformation, and Legacy" by Michael Stevens. This book has guided you on your path of faith and inspired you to grow closer to Christ.

Why Your Review Matters

YOUR FEEDBACK IS CRITICAL. By sharing your thoughts on this book, you're helping others decide if it's the right resource for them and contributing to a broader conversation about faith and transformation.

How to Leave a Review

WRITING a review doesn't have to be complicated. Here are some simple steps to guide you:

1. Click **the Book's Review Link:** https://www.amazon.com/review/create-review/?ie=UTF8&channel=glance-detail&asin=B0D5HBFQG8

. . .

2. Scan the QR Code:

~

What to Include in Your Review

- **Personal Experience:** How did the book help you? Share specific examples.
- **Favorite Sections:** Highlight the parts of the book that were most beneficial.
- **Practical Impact:** Describe how you've applied the lessons and the changes you've seen.
- **Recommendation:** Would you recommend this book to others? Why or why not?

Example Review

"I found 'How to Be Christlike' to be incredibly inspiring. The chapter on embracing forgiveness was a turning point for me. I've found a new sense of peace and connection with others by learning to forgive. The practical advice and heartfelt stories significantly impacted my faith journey. I highly recommend this book to anyone looking to deepen their relationship with Christ."

Your Impact

By leaving a review, you're making a difference. Your insights can help others find spiritual guidance and encourage more open discussions about faith and personal transformation.

Thank you for taking the time to share your experience. Your voice matters; your review can help others on their faith journey.

With gratitude,

Michael Stevens

~

CHAPTER 17

BEING A LIGHT IN THE WORLD

~

As followers of Christ, we are called to be a light in the world, reflecting His love, grace, and truth in every aspect of our lives. This chapter explores how to shine Christ's light in everyday situations, the influence of a Christlike life on others, and inspiring stories of transformation and impact.

. . .

Shining Christ's Light in Everyday Situations

Being a light in the world involves consistently living out our faith and reflecting Christ's character in all we do. This can be achieved through intentional actions, attitudes, and relationships.

Living with Integrity

Integrity is foundational to shining Christ's light. It involves honesty, trustworthiness, and consistency in our actions and words. By living with integrity, we demonstrate the reliability and truthfulness of Christ. Proverbs 11:3 emphasizes the importance of integrity: "The integrity of the upright guides them, but their duplicity destroys the unfaithful." Living with integrity in our personal and professional lives builds trust and credibility with others.

Demonstrating Love and Compassion

Christlike love and compassion are potent ways to shine His light in everyday situations. Jesus taught that loving our neighbors as ourselves is one of the greatest commandments (Matthew 22:39). By showing genuine care and concern for others, we reflect the love of Christ. This can be done through simple acts of kindness, listening to others, and offering support in times of need.

Exemplifying Humility and Service

HUMILITY AND SERVICE are critical characteristics of a Christlike life. Jesus demonstrated humility by washing His disciples' feet and serving others throughout His ministry (John 13:14-15). By putting the needs of others before our own and serving with a humble heart, we reflect the servant nature of Christ. This can be done through volunteering, helping those in need, and offering our time and talents to support others.

Practicing Forgiveness and Reconciliation

FORGIVENESS AND RECONCILIATION are central to the Gospel message. By practicing these virtues in our relationships, we demonstrate the power of God's grace and mercy. Ephesians 4:31-32 instructs, "Get rid of all bitterness, rage and anger, brawling and slander, along with every malice. Be kind and compassionate to one another, forgiving each other, just as in Christ God forgave you." By forgiving others and seeking reconciliation, we model the forgiveness we have received from Christ.

Displaying Joy and Peace

JOY AND PEACE are fruits of the Spirit that should be evident in the lives of believers. By displaying joy and peace, even under challenging circumstances, we testify to the sustaining power of God's presence. Philippians 4:4-7 encourages, "Rejoice in the Lord always. I will repeat it: Rejoice! Let your gentleness be evident to all. The Lord is near. Do not be anxious about anything, but in every situation, by prayer and petition, with thanksgiving, present your requests to God. And the peace of God, which transcends all understanding, will guard your hearts and minds in Christ Jesus." Living with joy and peace can attract others to our hope in Christ.

. . .

Engaging in Prayer

A PRAYER LIFE is essential for maintaining a close relationship with God and seeking His guidance in all aspects of life. By prioritizing prayer, we demonstrate our dependence on God and commitment to His will. 1 Thessalonians 5:16-18 instructs, "Rejoice always, pray continually, give thanks in all circumstances; for this is God's will for you in Christ Jesus." Consistent prayer strengthens our faith and sets an example for others to follow.

Cultivating a Spirit of Gratitude

GRATITUDE IS a powerful witness to God's goodness and faithfulness. By expressing gratitude daily, we reflect the joy and contentment of a relationship with Christ. 1 Thessalonians 5:18 encourages, "Give thanks in all circumstances; for this is God's will for you in Christ Jesus." Practicing gratitude can inspire others to seek the source of our joy and thankfulness.

Modeling Faithfulness

FAITHFULNESS IN OUR COMMITMENTS, relationships, and responsibilities demonstrates the reliability and trustworthiness of Christ. We build a strong testimony of God's faithfulness by being faithful in the small things. Luke 16:10 reminds us, "Whoever can be trusted with very little can also be trusted with much, and whoever is dishonest with very little will also be dishonest with much." Modeling faithfulness in all areas of our lives reflects the character of Christ and builds credibility with others.

. . .

Living a Life of Integrity

INTEGRITY in all aspects of life reflects the consistency and truthfulness of Christ's teachings. Living with integrity builds trust and respect with those around us. Proverbs 10:9 states, "Whoever walks in integrity walks securely, but whoever takes crooked paths will be found out." Living a life of integrity provides a strong witness to the Gospel's transformative power.

Practicing Generosity

GENEROSITY REFLECTS the heart of God and can be a powerful witness to His love and provision. We demonstrate the Gospel's transformative power by generously giving our time, resources, and talents. 2 Corinthians 9:6-7 encourages, "Remember this: Whoever sows sparingly will also reap sparingly, and whoever sows generously will also reap generously. Each of you should give what you have decided to give, not reluctantly or under compulsion, for God loves a cheerful giver." Generosity can touch lives and open doors for sharing the Gospel.

Influence of a Christlike Life on Others

A CHRISTLIKE LIFE has a profound impact on those around us. Our actions, attitudes, and relationships can influence others and draw them closer to Christ.

Building Trust and Credibility

Living a Christlike life builds trust and credibility with others. When people see that we consistently live out our faith with integrity and love, they are more likely to trust and respect us. This trust provides opportunities to share the Gospel and influence others for Christ.

Providing a Positive Example

Our lives serve as examples to others, whether we realize it or not. By living a Christlike life, we provide a positive example for others to follow. 1 Timothy 4:12 encourages, "Don't let anyone look down on you because you are young, but set an example for the believers in speech, conduct, love, faith, and purity." Our example can inspire others to seek Christ and live out their faith more fully.

Creating Opportunities for Conversations

Living a Christlike life often creates opportunities for conversations about faith. When others see Christ's difference in our lives, they may be curious and ask questions. 1 Peter 3:15 instructs, "But in your hearts revere Christ as Lord. Always be prepared to answer everyone who asks you to explain your hope. But do this with gentleness and respect." Preparing to share our faith and answer questions can lead to meaningful conversations and opportunities to share the Gospel.

Encouraging and Supporting Others

A Christlike life encourages and supports others in their faith journey. By offering encouragement, praying for others, and providing support in times of need, we reflect the love of Christ and help others grow in their faith. Hebrews 10:24-25 reminds us, "And let us consider how we may spur one another on toward love and good deeds, not giving up meeting together, as some are in the habit of doing, but encouraging one another—and all the more as you see the Day approaching." Encouraging and supporting others can strengthen their faith and deepen their relationship with Christ.

Being a Source of Hope and Inspiration

A CHRISTLIKE LIFE serves as a source of hope and inspiration for others. When people see how we handle challenges, exhibit joy, and demonstrate love, they may be inspired to seek the same qualities in their lives. Philippians 2:14-15 encourages, "Do everything without grumbling or arguing, so that you may become blameless and pure, 'children of God without fault in a warped and crooked generation.' Then you will shine among them like stars in the sky." By shining as lights in the world, we can inspire others to seek Christ and experience the hope and joy of a relationship with Him.

Stories of Transformation and Impact

STORIES OF TRANSFORMATION and impact highlight the power of a Christlike life and its influence on others. These stories inspire us to live out our faith and shine Christ's light in the world.

STORY 1: The Power of Forgiveness
Sarah had always struggled with bitterness and resentment

towards her father, who had abandoned their family when she was young. As she grew in her faith, she felt convicted to forgive him. Through prayer and the support of her church community, Sarah found the strength to reach out to her father and offer forgiveness. This forgiveness brought Sarah healing and opened the door for reconciliation with her father. Her willingness to forgive and demonstrate Christ's love profoundly impacted her family and inspired others in her church to pursue reconciliation in their relationships.

Story 2: A Life of Service

John had always been passionate about helping others. After coming to faith in Christ, he felt called to serve the homeless community in his city. John started a weekly outreach program, providing meals, clothing, and support to those in need. His dedication and compassion touched the lives of many and led several people to Christ. Through his acts of service, John demonstrated the love of Christ and made a lasting impact on his community.

Story 3: Living with Integrity

Emily worked in a corporate environment where unethical practices were standard. Despite the pressure to conform, she chose to live with integrity and uphold her Christian values. Emily's honesty and ethical behavior earned her the respect of her colleagues and superiors. Over time, several coworkers approached her to learn more about her faith and the principles that guided her actions. Through her example, Emily was able to share the Gospel and influence others to pursue integrity and honesty in their own lives.

· · ·

Story 4: Transforming a Community

Pastor James felt a burden for the struggling community surrounding his church. He mobilized his congregation to start various community programs, including after-school tutoring, job training, and health clinics. These initiatives addressed the community's physical, educational, and emotional needs and demonstrated the love of Christ in practical ways. The impact of these programs led to significant improvements in the community's well-being and opened doors for sharing the Gospel. Many lives were transformed, and the church became a beacon of hope and light in the neighborhood.

Story 5: Overcoming Adversity

Michael faced significant adversity after losing his job and experiencing financial hardship. Despite the challenges, he remained steadfast and trusted God's provision. Michael's unwavering faith and positive attitude inspired those around him, including his family and friends. His testimony of resilience and trust in God during difficult times encouraged others to seek God's strength and guidance in their struggles. Michael's story of overcoming adversity and maintaining faith had a ripple effect, leading many to experience the transformative power of Christ in their lives.

Story 6: The Influence of Joy and Peace

Lisa was known for her joyful and peaceful demeanor, even in the face of personal challenges. Her colleagues often wondered how she could maintain such a positive outlook. Lisa used these opportunities to share her faith and the source of her joy and peace—her relationship with Christ. Her consistent display of joy and peace attracted many to seek the same sense of fulfillment and contentment. Lisa's influence led to several of her colleagues attending church with her and eventually coming to faith in Christ. Her story illustrates the powerful impact of living a Christlike life and reflecting His joy and peace in everyday situations.

Story 7: Impact Through Mentorship

David felt called to mentor young men in his community, many facing challenging life circumstances. He provided guidance and support through his mentorship program and was a positive role model for these young men. David's Christlike character and dedication to their growth had a transformative impact on their lives. Many of the young men he mentored went on to pursue higher education, stable careers, and meaningful relationships with Christ. David's commitment to mentorship demonstrated the profound influence one person can have by living out their faith and investing in others.

Story 8: Spreading Hope in Crisis

During a natural disaster, Maria's community was devastated by loss and destruction. Amid the crisis, Maria organized relief efforts, bringing together resources and volunteers to support those affected. Her unwavering faith and compassionate response provided hope and comfort to many. Maria's actions not only met physical needs but also opened opportunities to share the hope of the Gospel. Her community witnessed the tangible expression of Christ's love; many were drawn to seek a relationship with Him. Maria's story highlights the impact of being a light in the world during times of crisis and need.

. . .

EVERY BELIEVER IS CALLED to be a light in the world. By shining Christ's light in everyday situations, living a Christlike life, and sharing inspiring stories of transformation and impact, we can influence others and draw them closer to Christ. We reflect Christ's love, grace, and truth to a needy world through intentional actions, attitudes, and relationships.

CHAPTER 18

BUILDING A CHRISTLIKE LEGACY

∾

Building a Christlike legacy involves living so that our faith and values influence our immediate circle and future generations. It is about creating a lasting impact through our actions, relationships, and dedication to mentoring and disciplining others. This chapter explores the long-term effects of

Christlike living, the importance of mentoring and disciplining others, and how to leave a legacy of faith.

Long-term Impact of Christlike Living

LIVING a Christlike life has a profound and enduring impact on those around us. It shapes our families, communities, and even society at large. Understanding the long-term effects of Christlike living motivates us to be intentional in our daily actions and decisions.

Influencing Family and Future Generations

OUR FAMILIES ARE the primary context in which our legacy is built. By living a Christlike life, we influence our children and grandchildren, passing on values, beliefs, and traditions that can endure for generations. Proverbs 22:6 highlights the importance of this influence: "Start children off on the way they should go, and even when they are old, they will not turn from it."

Creating a Culture of Faith in the Home

CREATING a culture of faith in the home involves regular family devotions, prayer, and religious discussions. By making faith a central part of family life, we instill in our children a strong foundation that will guide them throughout their lives. Deuteronomy 6:6-7 instructs, "These commandments that I give you today are to be on your hearts. Impress them on your children. Talk about them when you sit at home, walk along the road, lie down, and get up."

Modeling Christlike Behavior

CHILDREN LEARN by observing the behavior of their parents and other influential adults' behavior. By modeling Christlike behavior—such as honesty, kindness, forgiveness, and humility—we provide a tangible example for our children to emulate. This modeling reinforces the values we teach and helps our children understand what it means to live out their faith.

Building Strong Marriages

A ROBUST AND Christ-centered marriage sets a powerful example for children and others. Couples can show how faith influences their relationship and creates a stable and nurturing environment by demonstrating love, respect, and mutual support. Ephesians 5:25-28 instructs, "Husbands, love your wives, just as Christ loved the church and gave himself up for her to make her holy, cleansing her by the washing with water through the word, and to present her to himself as a radiant church, without stain or wrinkle or any other blemish, but holy and blameless. In this same way, husbands should love their wives as their bodies. He who loves his wife loves himself."

Impacting the Community

CHRISTLIKE LIVING EXTENDS beyond the family to the broader community. By being active and engaged members of our communities, we can significantly impact the lives of others. This involves volunteering, participating in community events, and supporting local initiatives. Our actions and involvement demonstrate the love of Christ and can inspire others to explore and embrace faith.

. . .

Demonstrating Ethical and Moral Leadership

Living a Christlike life in professional settings means demonstrating ethical and moral leadership. By conducting ourselves with integrity, fairness, and compassion, we set a standard for others to follow. This can influence workplace culture, promote ethical business practices, and create an environment where values and principles are prioritized.

Engaging in Social Justice

Christlike living also involves advocating for social justice and standing up for the marginalized and oppressed. Jesus' ministry was marked by compassion for the poor, the sick, and the outcasts. By following His example, we can work to address systemic injustices and promote equality and dignity for all people. Micah 6:8 reminds us, "He has shown you, O mortal, what is good. And what does the Lord require of you? Act justly, love mercy, and walk humbly with your God."

Leaving a Legacy Through Service

Service is a critical component of Christlike living. We create a lasting impact that can influence future generations by dedicating our time, talents, and resources to serving others. This can include participating in mission trips, supporting charitable organizations, and participating in church ministries. Acts 20:35 encourages us, "In everything I did, I showed you that by this kind of hard work, we must help the weak, remembering the words the Lord Jesus himself said: 'It is more blessed to give than to receive.'"

Mentoring and Discipling Others

MENTORING and disciplining others is a vital part of building a Christlike legacy. By investing in their spiritual growth and development, we multiply our impact and ensure that the values and teachings of Christ continue to spread.

Understanding the Role of a Mentor

A MENTOR PROVIDES GUIDANCE, support, and encouragement to help others grow spiritually and personally. Mentoring involves sharing wisdom, experiences, and insights to help the mentee navigate challenges and develop their faith. Proverbs 27:17 illustrates the value of mentorship: "As iron sharpens iron, so one person sharpens another."

Biblical Examples of Mentoring

THE BIBLE PROVIDES numerous examples of mentoring relationships. Moses mentored Joshua, preparing him to lead the Israelites into the Promised Land (Deuteronomy 34:9). Elijah mentored Elisha, passing on his prophetic ministry (2 Kings 2:9-15). Paul mentored Timothy, equipping him for pastoral leadership (2 Timothy 2:2). These examples highlight the importance of mentoring in spiritual development and leadership.

Identifying Potential Mentees

IDENTIFYING potential mentees involves recognizing individuals seeking to grow in their faith and being open to guidance and support. This can include young adults, new believers, or anyone facing significant life transitions. By being attentive to the needs and aspirations of others, we can identify those who would benefit from a mentoring relationship.

Building Trust and Relationship

A SUCCESSFUL MENTORING relationship is built on trust and mutual respect. This involves being reliable, maintaining confidentiality, and showing genuine care and concern for the mentee. Building a solid relationship creates a safe and supportive environment for the mentee to explore their faith and personal growth.

Setting Goals and Expectations

SETTING clear goals and expectations helps to provide direction and focus for the mentoring relationship. This can include specific spiritual disciplines, areas of personal growth, or life skills that the mentee wants to develop. By setting goals together, the mentor and mentee can work collaboratively towards achieving them.

Providing Guidance and Accountability

MENTORS GUIDE by sharing their experiences, offering advice, and helping the mentee navigate challenges. Accountability is also a key component of mentoring. By holding the mentee accountable to their goals and commitments, the mentor helps to ensure that progress is made and that the mentee stays on track.

Encouraging Spiritual Practices

ENCOURAGING the mentee to develop and maintain spiritual practices is essential to mentoring. These include regular prayer, Bible study, worship, and fellowship. By fostering these habits, the mentor helps the mentee grow closer to God and develop a strong foundation for their faith.

Celebrating Successes and Milestones

CELEBRATING successes and milestones is an essential aspect of mentoring. Recognizing the mentee's achievements and progress reinforces their efforts and motivates them to continue growing. Celebrations can include acknowledging answered prayers, spiritual breakthroughs, and personal accomplishments.

Continuing the Mentoring Relationship

MENTORING RELATIONSHIPS CAN EVOLVE, with the mentee eventually becoming a mentor to others. This multiplication effect ensures that the impact of the original mentoring relationship continues to spread. By encouraging mentees to become mentors themselves, we can create a legacy of discipleship that extends far beyond our influence.

Leaving a Legacy of Faith

LEAVING a legacy of faith involves intentionally living so that our influence endures long after we are gone. This requires focusing on life's spiritual, relational, and practical aspects.

Cultivating a Deep Personal Faith

A LEGACY of faith begins with cultivating a deep and personal relationship with God. This involves regular spiritual practices such as prayer, Bible study, worship, and reflection. By nurturing our faith, we create a strong foundation for influencing others.

Sharing Our Faith Story

SHARING our faith story is a powerful way to leave a legacy. This involves recounting how we came to faith, how God has worked in our lives, and the lessons we have learned. Our testimonies can inspire and encourage others in their faith journeys.

Documenting Spiritual Insights and Experiences

DOCUMENTING our spiritual insights and experiences through writing, journaling, or recording can provide valuable resources for future generations. These records can serve as a source of wisdom, guidance, and encouragement for our descendants and others who seek to learn from our experiences.

Creating Faith-based Traditions

CREATING faith-based traditions within our families and communities helps to reinforce values and beliefs. These traditions can include regular family devotions, holiday celebrations that focus on spiritual significance, and community service projects. Establishing these traditions creates opportunities for ongoing spiritual growth and connection.

Investing in the Next Generation

INVESTING in the next generation involves actively supporting and nurturing the spiritual development of younger individuals. This can include mentoring, teaching, and providing opportunities for young people to engage in ministry and service. Investing in the next generation ensures that our legacy of faith continues to thrive.

Supporting Faith-based Organizations

SUPPORTING faith-based organizations through financial contributions, volunteering, and advocacy helps to further the mission of spreading the Gospel and serving those in need. By partnering with these organizations, we can extend our impact and contribute to the growth and development of the Christian community.

Living with Purpose and Intention

LIVING PURPOSEFULLY MEANS ALIGNING our actions and decisions with our faith and values. It involves being intentional about how we spend our time, resources, and energy. We create a meaningful and impactful legacy by living with a clear sense of purpose.

. . .

Encouraging Stewardship and Generosity

ENCOURAGING stewardship and generosity involves teaching others the importance of managing resources wisely and giving generously. This can include financial stewardship, environmental stewardship, and using our talents and gifts to serve others. We create a culture of generosity and responsibility by modeling and teaching these principles.

Fostering a Spirit of Unity and Collaboration

FOSTERING a spirit of unity and collaboration within our families, churches, and communities helps to build a solid and supportive network of believers. This involves promoting teamwork, encouraging mutual support, and working together towards common goals. By fostering unity and collaboration, we create an environment where faith can flourish and grow.

Leaving a Lasting Impact through Acts of Kindness

SIMPLE ACTS of kindness can leave a lasting impact on others. By consistently demonstrating kindness and compassion, we create a ripple effect that can influence many lives. Acts of kindness can include helping a neighbor, supporting a friend in need, or showing appreciation to those who serve us. These small gestures can have a profound and enduring impact.

Living Out the Fruit of the Spirit

THE FRUIT OF THE SPIRIT—LOVE, joy, peace, forbearance, kindness, goodness, faithfulness, gentleness, and self-control (Galatians 5:22-23)—is evidence of a life transformed by Christ. By intentionally cultivating these qualities, we provide a living testament to the power of the Holy Spirit at work within us. These attributes influence how we interact with others and leave a lasting impression of God's love and character.

Engaging in Lifelong Learning and Growth

COMMITMENT to lifelong learning and personal growth is essential for maintaining a dynamic and impactful faith. This includes studying Scripture, seeking theological education, and being open to new insights and understanding. Proverbs 4:7 advises, "The beginning of wisdom is this: Get wisdom. Though it cost all you have, get understanding." A commitment to continuous learning ensures that our faith remains vibrant and relevant.

Leaving a Financial Legacy

PLANNING for the future through wills, trusts, and other financial instruments can ensure that our resources continue to support the work of the Kingdom after we are gone. This might include leaving funds to churches, Christian organizations, or ministries that align with our values. Proverbs 13:22 reminds us, "A good person leaves an inheritance for their children's children, but a sinner's wealth is stored up for the righteous."

Being an Advocate for Justice and Mercy

CHAMPIONING causes of justice and mercy is a critical aspect of a Christlike legacy. This involves standing up for the oppressed, working to correct injustices, and promoting policies that reflect biblical values of fairness and compassion. Isaiah 1:17 calls us to action: "Learn to do right; seek justice. Defend the oppressed. Take up the fatherless's cause; plead the widow's case." Advocacy work leaves a lasting impact by contributing to systemic change and fostering a more just society.

Writing and Sharing Wisdom

WRITING BOOKS, articles, or blogs on faith topics allows us to share our insights and experiences with a broader audience. These writings can serve as a lasting resource for others seeking to grow in their faith. By sharing our wisdom, we extend our influence beyond our immediate circle and contribute to the collective knowledge and understanding of the Christian faith.

Leaving a Legacy of Prayer

A LIFE CHARACTERIZED by prayer can leave a powerful legacy. This involves praying regularly for our family, friends, community, and the world. By establishing a pattern of intercessory prayer, we can influence the spiritual trajectory of those around us. 1 Thessalonians 5:17 encourages us to "pray continually." A legacy of prayer demonstrates our reliance on God and our commitment to seeking His will in all things.

Creating Enduring Institutions

ESTABLISHING or supporting institutions such as schools, hospitals, and community centers founded on Christian principles can have a lasting impact. These institutions can continue to serve and influence others long after we are gone. By contributing to the creation and sustenance of such institutions, we ensure that our values and beliefs are perpetuated in tangible ways.

Living with Joy and Hope

A LIFE MARKED by joy and hope is a powerful witness to the Gospel's transformative power. By maintaining a positive outlook and trusting in God's promises, we inspire others to seek the same joy and hope in their own lives. Romans 15:13 offers a prayer for this kind of life: "May the God of hope fill you with all joy and peace as you trust in him, so that you may overflow with hope by the power of the Holy Spirit." Living with joy and hope leaves a legacy that draws others to the source of our strength and contentment.

BUILDING a Christlike legacy involves living with intention, investing in the spiritual growth of others, and creating a lasting impact through our actions and relationships. By understanding the long-term effects of Christlike living, mentoring and disciplining others, and leaving a legacy of faith, we can ensure that our influence endures for future generations.

∽

CHAPTER 19
CONTINUING THE JOURNEY

~

The journey toward Christlikeness is a lifelong commitment that requires dedication, perseverance, and an ever-deepening relationship with God. This chapter explores the importance of this commitment, encourages the ongoing journey, and offers final reflections and prayers to support believers as they continue to grow in their faith.

～

Lifelong Commitment to Christlikeness

～

Understanding the Call to Christlikeness

THE CALL to Christlikeness is not a one-time event but a continuous transformation process. It involves striving to reflect the character, attitudes, and actions of Jesus in every aspect of our lives. Romans 12:2 emphasizes this ongoing transformation: "Do not conform to the pattern of this world but be transformed by renewing your mind. Then you can test and approve God's will—his good, pleasing, and perfect will." This transformation is a work of the Holy Spirit, who empowers us to grow in holiness and maturity.

The Role of Spiritual Disciplines

SPIRITUAL DISCIPLINES ARE essential for nurturing our relationship with God and fostering Christlikeness. These disciplines include prayer, Bible study, worship, fasting, and service. Regular engagement in these practices helps to cultivate a deeper connection with God and aligns our hearts with His will. 1 Timothy 4:7b-8 encourages us to "train yourself to be godly. Physical training is valuable, but godliness has value for all things, holding promise for both the present life and the life to come."

Embracing Continuous Growth

THE JOURNEY toward Christlikeness is marked by continuous growth and development. It involves recognizing that we will never fully arrive but always have areas where we can grow and improve. Philippians 3:12-14 captures this mindset: "Not that I have already obtained all this, or have already arrived at my goal, but I press on to take hold of that for which Christ Jesus took hold of me. Brothers and sisters, I do not consider myself yet to have taken hold of it. But one thing I do: Forgetting what is behind and straining toward what is ahead, I press on toward the goal to win the prize for which God has called me heavenward in Christ Jesus."

Persevering Through Challenges

THE JOURNEY toward Christlikeness has challenges and setbacks. We will face temptations, trials, and periods of doubt. However, perseverance is critical to overcoming these obstacles and growing in our faith. James 1:2-4 reminds us, "Consider it pure joy, my brothers and sisters, whenever you face trials of many kinds, because you know that testing your faith produces perseverance. Let perseverance finish its work so you may be mature and complete, not lacking anything." By trusting in God's strength and relying on His grace, we can persevere through difficulties and continue our journey toward Christlikeness.

The Importance of Community

COMMUNITY PLAYS a vital role in our journey toward Christlikeness. Fellow believers provide support, encouragement, and accountability, helping us to stay on track and grow in our faith. Hebrews

10:24-25 highlights the importance of community: "And let us consider how we may spur one another on toward love and good deeds, not giving up meeting together, as some are in the habit of doing, but encouraging one another—and all the more as you see the Day approaching." Engaging with a faith community through church involvement, small groups, and fellowship helps to strengthen our commitment to Christlikeness.

Seeking God's Guidance

A LIFELONG COMMITMENT to Christlikeness involves continually seeking God's guidance and direction. This requires a posture of humility and openness to the leading of the Holy Spirit. Proverbs 3:5-6 encourages us, "Trust in the Lord with all your heart and lean not on your understanding; in all your ways submit to him, and he will make your paths straight." By seeking God's guidance through prayer and Scripture, we can discern His will and make decisions that align with His purposes.

~

Encouragement for the Ongoing Journey

~

Finding Strength in God's Promises

GOD'S PROMISES provide strength and encouragement for our journey toward Christlikeness. Scripture is filled with assurances of God's presence, provision, and faithfulness. Isaiah 41:10 offers comfort: "So do not fear, for I am with you; do not be dismayed, for I am your God. I will strengthen, help, and uphold you with my righteous right hand." By meditating on God's promises, we can find the strength to persevere and remain steadfast in our commitment.

Embracing Grace and Forgiveness

AS WE PURSUE CHRISTLIKENESS, we will inevitably fall short and make mistakes. Embracing God's grace and forgiveness is essential for moving forward and continuing our growth. 1 John 1:9 assures us, "If we confess our sins, he is faithful and just and will forgive us and purify us from all unrighteousness." Understanding that God forgives and loves us allows us to let go of guilt and shame and focus on becoming more like Christ.

Drawing Inspiration from Others

THE TESTIMONIES and examples of other believers can inspire and encourage us on our journey. By learning from the experiences of others, we can gain insights and motivation to continue growing in our faith. Hebrews 12:1-2 encourages us to look to the examples of those who have gone before us: "Therefore since such a great cloud of witnesses surrounds us, let us throw off everything that hinders and the sin that so easily entangles. And let us run with perseverance the race marked out for us, fixing our eyes on Jesus, the pioneer and perfecter of faith."

Practicing Gratitude

GRATITUDE IS an assertive attitude that can transform our perspective and fuel our commitment to Christlikeness. By focusing on the blessings and provisions God has given us, we can cultivate a heart of thankfulness and joy. 1 Thessalonians 5:16-18 instructs, "Rejoice always, pray continually, give thanks in all circumstances; for this is God's will for you in Christ Jesus." Practicing gratitude helps us to remain positive and motivated, even in the face of challenges.

Setting Spiritual Goals

SETTING spiritual goals provides direction and focus for our journey toward Christlikeness. These goals can include specific areas of personal growth, spiritual disciplines, or ways to serve others. Setting and pursuing these goals creates a roadmap for our spiritual development. Philippians 3:13-14 encourages us to press on toward our goals: "Brothers and sisters, I do not consider myself yet to have taken hold of it. But one thing I do: Forgetting what is behind and straining toward what is ahead, I press on toward the goal to win the prize for which God has called me heavenward in Christ Jesus."

Cultivating a Prayerful Life

PRAYER IS a vital component of our spiritual journey, providing a direct line of communication with God. By cultivating prayer, we can seek God's guidance, express our needs and desires, and develop a deeper relationship with Him. Philippians 4:6-7 encourages us, "Do not be anxious about anything, but in every situation, by prayer and petition, with thanksgiving, present your requests to God. And the peace of God, which transcends all understanding, will guard your hearts and minds in Christ Jesus." A consistent prayer life helps us to stay connected to God and aligned with His will.

Engaging in Regular Bible Study

REGULAR BIBLE STUDY is essential for understanding and applying God's word to our lives. By studying Scripture, we gain insights into God's character, promises, and instructions for living a Christlike life. Psalm 119:105 declares, "Your word is a lamp for my feet, a light on my path." Regular Bible study helps us grow in our knowledge of God and equips us to live out our faith.

Seeking Wisdom and Counsel

SEEKING wisdom and counsel from trusted mentors, pastors, and fellow believers can provide valuable insights and guidance for our journey. Proverbs 19:20 advises, "Listen to advice and accept discipline, and at the end, you will be counted among the wise." By seeking counsel, we can gain perspective, receive encouragement, and make informed decisions that align with God's will.

Finding Joy in the Journey

THE JOURNEY toward Christlikeness is not just about the destination but also about finding joy. By embracing the growth and transformation along the way, we can experience the fullness of life God intends for us. John 10:10b reminds us, "I have come that they may have life, and have it to the full." Finding joy in the journey helps us to stay motivated and engaged in our spiritual development.

~

Final Reflections and Prayers

Reflecting on God's Faithfulness

As we continue our journey toward Christlikeness, we must reflect on God's faithfulness and how He has worked in our lives. By remembering His provision, guidance, and blessings, we can find encouragement and motivation to persevere. Lamentations 3:22-23 reminds us, "Because of the Lord's great love we are not consumed, for his compassions never fail. They are new every morning; great is your faithfulness." Reflecting on God's faithfulness helps us trust His ongoing presence and support.

Committing to Ongoing Growth

Committing to ongoing growth involves seeking God's guidance and pursuing spiritual development. This requires humility, openness to change, and a desire to become more like Christ. Philippians 1:6 offers assurance of God's ongoing work in our lives: "Being confident of this, that he who began a good work in you will carry it on to completion until the day of Christ Jesus." By committing to ongoing growth, we acknowledge that our journey is a lifelong process of becoming more like Christ.

Prayer for Strength and Guidance

Heavenly Father, we thank You for Your faithfulness and the work You do in our lives. As we continue our journey toward Christlikeness, we ask for Your strength and guidance. Please help us remain steadfast in our commitment and persevere through challenges. Fill us with Your Holy Spirit, and guide us in all we do. May our lives reflect Your love, grace, and truth, and may we bring glory to Your name. In Jesus' name, we pray. Amen.

Prayer for Wisdom and Discernment

LORD, we seek Your wisdom and discernment as we navigate life's challenges and decisions. Grant us clarity and understanding, and help us align our actions with Your will. Surround us with wise counsel and a supportive community to guide our spiritual growth. May we be attentive to Your leading and open to Your guidance. In Jesus' name, we pray. Amen.

Prayer for Joy and Peace

GRACIOUS GOD, we thank You for the joy and peace of knowing You. Please help us embrace these gifts and find contentment in our journey. May we be a source of joy and peace to others, reflecting Your love and grace in all we do. Fill our hearts with gratitude, and help us focus on Your blessings. In Jesus' name, we pray. Amen.

Prayer for Community and Support

FATHER, we thank You for the gift of community and the support of fellow believers. Please help us build strong, Christ-centered relationships that encourage and uplift one another. May we spur one another toward love and good deeds, and may our community be a beacon of Your love and truth. Guide us as we support and mentor others and help us create a lasting impact. In Jesus' name, we pray. Amen.

Final Reflections

As we conclude this journey toward Christlikeness, we are reminded of the profound and transformative impact that a life devoted to following Jesus can have. Committing to Christlikeness is a lifelong endeavor marked by continuous growth, perseverance, and reliance on God's grace. We can grow and become more like Christ by embracing spiritual disciplines, seeking community, and reflecting on God's faithfulness.

The journey is not without challenges, but with God's strength and guidance, we can overcome obstacles and remain steadfast in our commitment. We are called to be a light in the world, reflecting Christ's love, grace, and truth in all we do. Living out our faith leaves a lasting legacy that influences our families, communities, and future generations.

Let us commit to ongoing growth, seek God's guidance, and find joy in the journey. May our lives be a testament to the Gospel's transformative power and bring glory to God in all we do.

Final Prayers

Heavenly Father, we thank You for the journey You have set before us. As we strive to become more like Christ, we ask for Your strength, guidance, and grace. Help us persevere through challenges and remain steadfast in our commitment to You. May our lives reflect Your love, grace, and truth, and may we bring glory to Your name. In Jesus' name, we pray. Amen.

. . .

LORD, we seek Your wisdom and discernment as we navigate the path of Christlikeness. Grant us clarity and understanding, and help us to align our actions with Your will. Surround us with a supportive community and guide us in our spiritual growth. May we be attentive to Your leading and open to Your guidance. In Jesus' name, we pray. Amen.

GRACIOUS GOD, we thank You for the joy and peace of knowing You. Please help us embrace these gifts and find contentment in our journey. May we be a source of joy and peace to others, reflecting Your love and grace in all we do. Fill our hearts with gratitude, and help us focus on Your blessings. In Jesus' name, we pray. Amen.

FATHER, we thank You for the gift of community and the support of fellow believers. Please help us build strong, Christ-centered relationships that encourage and uplift one another. May we spur one another toward love and good deeds, and may our community be a beacon of Your love and truth. Guide us as we support and mentor others and help us create a lasting impact. In Jesus' name, we pray. Amen.

AS WE CONTINUE our journey toward Christlikeness, let us do so with a heart full of gratitude, a spirit of perseverance, and a deep reliance on God's grace. May we continually seek His guidance, embrace His love, and reflect His character in all we do. May our lives be a testimony to the Gospel's transformative power, bringing glory to God and inspiring others to follow Him. Amen.

∾

CHAPTER 20

BOOK REVIEW REQUEST

Make a Difference with Your Review

Unlock the Power of Generosity

"Giving is not just about donating. It is about making a difference." - Kathy Calvin.

∼

DEAR READER,

Thank you for choosing "How to Be Christlike: A Journey of Faith, Transformation, and Legacy" by Michael Stevens. This book has guided you on your path of faith and inspired you to grow closer to Christ.

Why Your Review Matters

YOUR FEEDBACK IS CRITICAL. By sharing your thoughts on this book, you're helping others decide if it's the right resource for them and contributing to a broader conversation about faith and transformation.

How to Leave a Review

WRITING a review doesn't have to be complicated. Here are some simple steps to guide you:

1. Click **the Book's Review Link:** https://www.amazon.com/review/create-review/?ie=UTF8&channel=glance-detail&asin=B0D5HBFQG8

. . .

2. Scan the QR Code:

∽

What to Include in Your Review

- **Personal Experience:** How did the book help you? Share specific examples.
- **Favorite Sections:** Highlight the parts of the book that were most beneficial.
- **Practical Impact:** Describe how you've applied the lessons and the changes you've seen.
- **Recommendation:** Would you recommend this book to others? Why or why not?

Example Review

"I found 'How to Be Christlike' to be incredibly inspiring. The chapter on embracing forgiveness was a turning point for me. I've found a new sense of peace and connection with others by learning to forgive. The practical advice and heartfelt stories significantly impacted my faith journey. I highly recommend this book to anyone looking to deepen their relationship with Christ."

Your Impact

By leaving a review, you're making a difference. Your insights can help others find spiritual guidance and encourage more open discussions about faith and personal transformation.

Thank you for taking the time to share your experience. Your voice matters; your review can help others on their faith journey.

With gratitude,

Michael Stevens

BIBLIOGRAPHY

New International Version. (2011). *The Holy Bible*. Zondervan.
Romans 12:2, New International Version)
(1 Timothy 4:7b-8, New International Version)
(Philippians 3:12-14, New International Version)
(James 1:2-4, New International Version)
(Hebrews 10:24-25, New International Version)
(Proverbs 3:5-6, New International Version)
(Isaiah 41:10, New International Version)
(1 John 1:9, New International Version)
(Hebrews 12:1-2, New International Version)
(1 Thessalonians 5:16-18, New International Version)
(Philippians 4:6-7, New International Version)
(Psalm 119:105, New International Version)
(Proverbs 19:20, New International Version)
(John 10:10b, New International Version)
(Lamentations 3:22-23, New International Version)
(Philippians 1:6, New International Version)

ABOUT THE AUTHOR

~

Michael Stevens, the esteemed author of "How to Be Christlike: A Journey of Faith, Transformation, and Legacy," is a renowned theologian and spiritual guide. With a profound understanding of Christian theology and a passion for exploring the intricacies of faith, Stevens has dedicated his career to helping others reflect the character and teachings of Jesus Christ in their daily lives.

Throughout his career, Michael Stevens has been unwavering in his commitment to fostering greater understanding and dialogue across religious and cultural boundaries. His work is a testament to his dedication to empathy, respect, and intellectual rigor as he seeks to illuminate the shared values and aspirations that unite humanity in its quest for meaning and purpose.

As a prolific writer, Stevens brings a wealth of knowledge and experience to his exploration of Christlike living. His unique ability to blend scholarly research with accessible language ensures that his work is enlightening and engaging for readers of all backgrounds, from seasoned theologians to those new to the faith.

Beyond his literary contributions, Stevens is a respected speaker and educator known for his dynamic presentations and thought-provoking lectures on faith and spirituality. His genuine passion for sharing wisdom and guiding others on their spiritual journeys has earned him a reputation as a trusted voice in Christian theology.

Through "How to Be Christlike: A Journey of Faith, Transformation, and Legacy," Michael Stevens invites readers on a transformative journey of discovery. His book offers profound insights and guidance, catalyzing those seeking to deepen their relationship with Christ. With clarity, compassion, and wisdom, Stevens illuminates the path to a richer, more meaningful life in alignment with Jesus's teachings.

ALSO BY MICHAEL STEVENS

~

"Vivir como Cristo": Un viaje de fe, transformación y legado (Spanish Edition)

"Cómo ser semejante a Cristo": Un viaje de fe, transformación y legado (Spanish Edition)

"Estranged Relationships: What Can Be Done - Is There Anything to Be Done?"

"Understanding Christianity: Exploring the Depths of Faith"

"Exploring Christianity: A Journey of Understanding"

"How to Be Christlike: A Journey of Faith, Transformation, and Legacy"

Living Christlike: A Journey of Faith, Transformation, and Legacy

Made in the USA
Middletown, DE
25 November 2024

65361996R00159